A
Balkan
Summer

George East

First Impressions: A Balkan Summer
Published by La Puce Publications
website: www.la-puce.co.uk

© George East 2017

This printing 2020

Typesetting and design by Bryony Parsons

Paperback first edition ISBN: 9781908747419
mobi-kindle version ISBN: 9781908747426
e-Pub version ISBN: 9781908747433

Other books by George East

Home & Dry in France
René & Me
French Letters
French Flea Bites
French Cricket
French Kisses
French Lessons

French Impressions: Brittany
French Impressions: The Loire Valley
French Impressions: The Dordogne River
French Impressions: Lower Normandy
French Impressions: 150 Fabulous French Recipes
French Impressions: The Brittany Blogs

Home & Dry in Normandy (compilation)
French Kisses (compilation)
Love Letters to France (French Collection)

Also:

A Year Behind Bars
How to write a Best-Seller
The Naked Truth about Women
The Naked Truth about Dieting
France and the French - How to Buy a Home in France

The Mowgley Crime series:

Death Duty
Deadly Tide
Dead Money
Death á la Carte
Dead and Buried

LA PUCE PUBLICATIONS

e-mail: lapucepublications@hotmail.co.uk.
website: **www.george-east.net**

About the author

Before becoming a proper writer, George East sampled a number of occupations. They included failed rock star, successful pickled onion manufacturer, seamstress, demolition engineer, private detective, night club bouncer, radio disc jockey and the world's only professional bed-tester. In his time as a publican, he was named as the *News of the World's* Worst Landlord in Britain for two consecutive years. The newspaper then scrapped the contest because they did not believe anyone else would ever challenge his obvious right to the title in perpetuity.

George now lives with his wife Donella on an Island off the south coast, and spends most of his year visiting other countries and writing about them. He is also the author of the Inspector Mowgley series, and has a backlog of book projects he estimates will last him until he reaches the age of 127. At least.

Common knowledge

A recent survey of fairly-well educated Britons revealed the extent of their knowledge about one of the newest members of the European Union. They confidently claimed that Bulgaria:

- is named after one of the Wombles
- is somewhere in Eastern Europe
- uses a funny alphabet
- is a very poor country
- has lots of mountains
- is where most of the assassins in the James Bond books come from

Most of these assertions are in fact, correct - except for the bit about the assassins, though they did feature largely in *From Russia with Love*.

Bulgaria is indeed in Eastern Europe, squeezed in between five countries and the Black Sea. Mighty Romania takes up the whole of the northern border, and Serbia and Macedonia share the western boundary. Greece and Turkey stop Bulgaria from falling into the Aegean Sea.

The fourteenth largest country on the continent of Europe, Bulgaria is a bit smaller than England, and at time of writing the ever-shrinking population stands at just below or just above seven million.

Whatever the precise figure at time of writing, Bulgaria is expected to have the most rapidly declining population in the *world* in the not-so-distant future.

Bulgaria joined the European Union in 2007, and so far three million Bulgars have chosen to work and live abroad. Most are young, and this helps explain the dramatic decline in population and birth rate. Their reasons for leaving Bulgaria may not be unconnected to the fact that it is one of the poorest countries in Europe.

Though tied to the Euro, the currency remains the lev, and the average wage is not much more than the equivalent of £300 a month compared to Britain's £2000.

Thirty percent of this beautiful country is covered in woodland, and the Balkan range runs from the border with Serbia eastwards to the Black Sea. The name of the range comes from ancient Persian, and in Bulgarian simply means 'mountain'.

The Balkans are crossed by twenty passes and two gorges, and the mountainous terrain has helped shape the country's history and destiny. Going anywhere can take a deal longer, which may explain why many Bulgarians drive as if they are criminally insane.

Famous Bulgarian figures include soccer star Dimitar Berbatov (Spurs, Manchester United and Fulham), *You Tube* star Baki the Snowman (pass) and, somewhat surprisingly, television's *Inspector Wexford* actor George Baker. It is also believed that the Thracian rebel role model Spartacus was a native of what was to become Bulgaria.

Finally, although I don't know who asked whom and what the questions and parameters were, Bulgaria is ranked at 144th out of the 156 countries in what is called The United Nations World Happiness Index (yes, I know).

Though it is not completely clear how the rankings were established, there is a clue in the fact that, believe it or not, the general rule is that the richer the country the happier its people.

Timeline

It is said that a nation's character is formed by its history, and in particular its occupation and treatment by foreign forces. If that is true, Bulgaria has more than a fair enough reason for scoring so low on the UN Happiness index. But to begin at the beginning:

1,000,000 years BC: Much evidence of occupation by early Stone Age cave-dwelling hunter-gatherers.

7000-5000 BC (approx): Arrival of the Thracians, who were of Indo-European origin, and said to be tall, fearless mercenaries. Amongst the most skilled gladiators in Ancient Rome, their numbers are said to have included Spartacus, the almost-successful 1st-century (BC) rebel leader.

4th century BC: Philip the Macedonian conquers the greater part of Thrace, and is followed by his son, Alexander the Great.

1st century BC: Rome takes over.

395 AD: The Roman Empire breaks into two. The eastern part has Constantinople as its capital, and Rome heads the western lands. Present-day Bulgarian territory remained within the eastern part and was known in the Middle Ages as Byzantium.

4th to 7th centuries: Devastating raids by Goths, Huns and Avars cause the Thracians to flee to the mountains. The first Bulgarian and Slav settlements appear on the Balkan Peninsula. The Bulgarian Empire is established in 681.

8th century: Bulgaria halts the Arab expansion into Europe, saving Byzantium.

9th century: Constantine the Philosopher (known to his mates as Cyril) and his brother Methodius complete the first Bulgarian and Slavonic alphabet, thereby creating frustration and distress for visiting tourists in times to come.

11th century: Gaining independence from Byzantine domination in 1186, medieval Bulgaria experiences a great political and cultural upsurge.

14th century: Bulgaria is invaded by the Ottoman Empire and horror ensues. Slaughter takes place on a monstrous scale and tens of thousands of Bulgarians are deported to Asia Minor. Christian temples are destroyed and genocide flourishes in the name of Islam. Numerous uprisings occur, but are, as was recorded, 'drowned in blood.'

19th century: The movement for national liberation grows, with Vassil Levski, 'The Apostle of Freedom' as its figurehead. The 1876 April Uprising is a turning point and its bloody crushing led to the Russo -Turkish War and liberation for Bulgaria in 1878.

20th century: The participation of Bulgaria in the First and Second World Wars is a catastrophic attempt at national unification, and they join the losing side on both occasions.

In 1944, the government of the Fatherland Front takes control and Bulgaria is proclaimed a Republic the following year. The Bulgarian Communist Party assumes power and all political parties except the Fatherland Front are banned.

Bulgaria remained part of the Eastern bloc until 1989, when comes the re-birth of democracy.

2007: Bulgaria becomes part of the European Union.

Regal footnote: With interruptions and under various names such as tsar, prince and khan, potentates ruled Bulgaria from the year 681 till 1946, when the monarchy was abolished in a referendum, allegedly rigged by the Communists.

Money matters

Bulgaria still uses its own currency (the lev*), but, as a member of the EU, is governed by a currency board which ties the value at a fixed rate to the Euro. Whatever happens in the crucible of currency exchange, there are always nearly two leva to the Euro. The lev is divided into 100 stotinki.

You will note that where I give prices in leva, I invariably follow-up with what that means in pounds or pennies sterling. This is not to gloat about how cheap things are in Bulgaria (or seem so to us) but to give an idea of comparative prices and values without you repeatedly having to do the sums.

At time of writing, the average wage in Bulgaria is less than the equivalent of £400 a month. In the UK it is more than five times that. Averages rarely mean much but they do give an insight into aspects of the cost of living in any country. In this respect, Bulgaria is awash with financial anomalies from a British perspective.

For instance, there is certainly no shortage of housing stock in Bulgaria, and a modest home may be had for the price of a new car in the UK - and sometimes for the price of an old one. On the other hand, domestic and what we usually call white goods may be as much as three-quarters of what you would expect to pay for them for in the UK. This makes them very dear for the average-income Bulgarian.

Shoes and clothing are also relatively expensive compared with what we are used to paying. So it is not just a case of expecting everything in Bulgaria to be a fraction of what it would cost in Britain. Some things seem so cheap they are almost jaw-dropping; others not so, especially if you, like the average Bulgar, are working for less than twenty quid a day.

In a time and land of plenty, it is hard for most of us to understand that the great majority of Bulgarians are on a very, very tight budget, however cheap things seem to we lucky Brits. That is of course why so many of them choose to come and work and live with us.

The currency was devalued in 1999 after massive inflation, when a thousand lev became just one. Don't think you have hit the jackpot if you are offered a leva note with lots of noughts on it, as they are now officially worthless.

PS. *I must also confess to have taken liberties with the Bulgarian language by spelling words as they sound rather than as they would appear in Cyrillic or sometimes in an English-Bulgarian dictionary. Thus 'donkey' is written as it is said - 'magare', rather than донкей or, as it would appear in most dictionaries, 'marape'.*

Health matters

- The average lifespan in Bulgaria is 71 years for men and 77 years for women. This is a great improvement on the figures at the end of the communist era. It is still one of the three lowest (i.e. worst) figures in the EU and compares with 78 and 82 years respectively in the UK. This is not as great a difference as you might have suspected, given some aspects of the Bulgarian cuisine and their enthusiasm for smoking. Perhaps not unsurprisingly given the so-called 'Mediterranean diet' the highest life expectancy in Euroland is enjoyed by Spain, Italy and France.

- At 15 percent, Bulgaria's mortality rate* is the worst of the 28 countries in the European Union. The country is also in the top twenty of world rankings for death from heart disease, hypertension and lung cancer. Thirty percent of Bulgarians die from coronary heart disease but, curiously, less than four percent from cancer of the lung. This is curious because the Bulgars are beaten only by the Greeks as the heaviest smokers in Europe. There has been a smoking ban in bars and workplaces and in or even near administrative buildings since 2012, but like speed limits, wearing crash helmets and driving with lights on, many Bulgarians regard it as not applying to them. Owners of many premises seem equally less bothered about upholding this law. While stickers informing visitors that guns are not allowed on the premises are common, I saw few non-smoking signs at the many bars I visited.

- Fifty eight percent of the population is overweight and 23 percent obese. This compares with an obesity rate of nearly 25 percent in Britain, showing that our national diet is even worse than theirs, and confirming us as what the media likes to call the 'Fat Man' of Europe.

- One in eight Bulgars has high blood pressure, and at the last reckoning there were around half a million diabetics. This might not sound much compared to the British tally of over three million, but it should be remembered that Bulgaria's population is not much more than a tenth of ours.

*the mortality rate of any country is the ratio of deaths expressed per thousand per year.

Author's Note

There are as usual too many people to thank for their help with this book, so I won't try.

For those who like to know these things, Krasiva is a real village, only with another name. Anyone with a guide book or map of north-western Bulgaria and references to the other places mentioned should not have a problem finding it. Similarly, all the characters and events featured in these pages are real, excepting those who are not.

I would also like to add that I went to Bulgaria to write a magazine article about an English couple's apparently daffy mission to resuscitate a mountain village - and came away completely smitten by a whole country and its people.

Blimey.

At about the same size and shape, the Easyjet cabin window reminds me of the screen of our first television set. What I see through it puts me in mind of the aerial newsreel shots of Stalingrad after the siege was lifted in 1944,

My view of the capital of Bulgaria is in colour and the dereliction on a much lesser scale, but it still looks pretty grim. The post - battle impression comes mostly from hundreds of skeletal structures amongst the legions of drab, apartment blocks.

But what look like bomb and shell-damaged buildings are in fact works in progress. Or rather, not in progress.

As a fellow passenger explains, it is not that Sofia is undergoing a construction boom; rather it is undergoing a construction freeze. Most of the structures are pagoda-style creations with floors and ceilings held apart by time and pollution-blackened concrete beams. Some have walls, but are eyeless and look as if they have been stripped by a repo company because materials have not been paid for.

As my informant says, each site will have its own story and reason for the cessation of work, but all the reasons will be to do with money.

Surrounding the abandoned building sites are hundreds

of clearly very occupied apartment blocks. They seem ironically festive, draped with lines of freshly-washed garments, and encircle the heart of the city like a besieging army of cubist giants. They are completely untroubled by any attempts to alleviate their severe functionality, date from the Communist era, and look it.

The plane is now low enough to see children playing amongst what looks like vast car breakers' yards surrounding many of the blocks. As we get lower, I see that most of the vehicles appear to be still in use.

According to my guide book, at over 500 metres above sea level Sofia is the highest capital city in Europe. It is also the capital of one of the poorest countries in Europe. Five out of the six provinces of Bulgaria are among the ten most deprived places in the EU. I am going to the poorest of all the regions to investigate what appears to be a completely bonkers scheme to revive a dying mountain village.

~

My first impressions of Bulgaria at ground level are much more pleasant. I don't know about the country yet, but the airport seems to be a refreshingly laid-back place; so much so that it has even affected the mood of travellers.

In Gatwick I was borne along by a manic horde, fighting their way to the departure gates as if they had an impatient train rather than static airplane to catch. As most of the frenetic mob would have had their seats booked and planes are not known for departing until at least the advertised time, I have never been able to work out why the customers act like it's a race, with the spoils to the victors.

But things at Sofia airport are clearly done differently. Even the most frenetic passengers I encountered at Gatwick have undergone a spiritual metamorphosis. There is little pushing or shoving to de-plane, and we almost saunter down the steps towards the buses. At the doors, a young couple even invite me to board before them. When I recover I, thank them and get on just before the doors hiss and close, leaving them stranded. Rather than rail and rant, they merely shrug, pick up their bags and walk off in the direction of the terminal. Perhaps they fancy stretching their legs after the three-hour flight; or perhaps they have heard about Bulgarian bus drivers.

~

The last time I arrived at Gatwick, less than half of the cubicles supposed to be personned by the Border Force were occupied. Several hundred people were fighting to find and join the shortest queue although there wasn't one.

At the Sofia terminal there are three boxes, and all have people sitting in them. Standing in front of them, a statuesque lady with big purple hair and in a uniform under severe stress is managing the queues. Given her size, she uses surprisingly elegant and dainty gestures to draw us on, and I am put in mind of a *tai-chi* enthusiast limbering up for a session. Extraordinarily for any airport I have used, nobody seems in a hurry, and it is almost like a line-up outside a West End theatre. They know the show won't start without them, so there is no need to push and shove or radiate anxiety and frustration. Queuing to get in is all part of the evening's fun.

As I near the front of the line, a baby at the back starts to cry and the purple-haired lady gestures to the mother to jump the queue. Nobody objects, and most of us smile indulgently as she passes.

Meanwhile, I pass the time chatting with my two neighbours on the flight.

Ivan and Yana come straight from the Handsome Young Slavic Couple register at central casting. He is very big and square, with hands like shovels. His head is close-cropped, and his cheekbones and eyebrows so prominent he looks like a long-time pugilist. Most noticeably, the Khrushchev-style baby-like snub nose looks lost in his broad, widely-planed face.

His partner is blonde with cheekbones and nose which would cost a fortune to have created cosmetically, as would her voluptuously full lips and firm chin. Looking at her, I think how so many eastern European women encompass our western ideals of classic beauty.

On the plane I learned that Yana is a nurse and Ivan works in the building trade in London. They are going back home for a holiday but do not expect to return permanently to Bulgaria, even when they retire. As they say, they have grown used to the pace of life and standard of living in London.

I nod to show I understand what they mean, and have already noticed how they have become used to the big earning and big spending levels in the UK. On the plane, I stuck to a bottle of water bought in a convenience store outside the airport and smuggled on board. The young couple ordered bacon rolls and coffee and chocolates from the stewardess, and the bill for their snack was around a day's wages in their home country; in fact, it was not much less than the cost of my flight to Sofia.

Ivan and Yana are just two of the millions of mostly young people who have left Bulgaria to find a better life, and I think their story is a common one. There is nothing for them in their home country, and the irony is that by leaving they have made the country even less attractive to people like them. More than half of all departed Bulgarians leave when under thirty, and on average they send no more than a few pounds home each year. Their lives, as Yana says with the beginnings of a sad smile, are now elsewhere.

I have heard and read some wildly differing estimates by Bulgarians about the size and significance of the exodus to other parts of Europe and the rest of the world. The figure varies depending on who you ask, but it is fairly certain that more Bulgarians are currently working elsewhere than in their own country. 2.5 million are employed abroad, while the total workforce at home is 2.2. million. The émigrés send around 1.7 million Euros home, which is not much of a boost to a lowly economy of 40 billion.

The migration began during the Communist years, and official statistics from the Bulgarian Foreign Ministry puts the figure at more than three million people, over half of whom are in their twenties. To put the situation into perspective, that would be like thirty-odd million young Britons leaving the UK to work abroad.

It is somewhat ironic that so many people in Britain worry about too many people moving in to their country, while Bulgarians left at home fear the virtual emptying of theirs.

I have exchanged e-mail addresses with my new friends and made the usual rarely-kept promises about keeping in touch, and am watching the unofficial entertainment from the airport coffee shop.

My hosts have arranged a cab and given the driver a photograph of me so that he will have no trouble finding me. I also need to sit down for a while to get over buying an espresso and a bar of chocolate at an international airport for the equivalent of 75 pence.

I like watching people passing through my life while I make guesses as to where they are going, why they are going there and what their lives are like. It is an undemanding game as I shall never know how right or wrong I am, so always believe myself to be right.

Today, the main show is provided by a couple of Special

Forces operatives, who should look intimidating in their ski masks, body armour, camouflage uniforms and with snub-nosed machine guns cradled in their arms. They are clearly here to reassure travellers after the terrorist outrage this morning at Istanbul airport, but are certainly not complying with the part of their job description which requires them to look menacingly competent.

One is well over six foot tall with a muscular build emphasised by his upper-body armour and close-fitting uniform. The other is more than a head shorter and looks like a child dressed up in an outfit made for a bigger boy. His Kevlar vest hangs limply on his upper half, and his camouflaged trousers concertina down over skinny legs to his almost clown-like oversized boots. He is Bobby Ball to his colleague's Tommy Cannon. He does not have any braces to snap, but makes the most of his ski mask as a gizmo, constantly pulling it up to make funny faces. He also keeps up a constant exchange with his colleague and the group of airport workers surrounding them, particularly a very attractive blonde stewardess. I don't know how the two men would react in the case of a terrorist attack, but it is somehow reassuring that they are so relaxed.

As the stewardess poses for a selfie with the masked warriors, I sense someone standing beside me. A hand appears in my field of vision. I look down and see myself as I was a long time ago. It is my official publicity photograph, and was taken more than a decade ago in a flattering light. In my and their defence, it is a common trick used by publishers in this youth-obsessed age.

The man holding the photograph is looking from it to me as he compares artifice with reality. He must think I have been ill lately, or had a very bad flight. I nod confirmation that I am me, and he smiles sympathetically and picks up my bag and leads the way from the café.

He is a small man with particularly short legs, but it is still a job to keep up with him. From his movements and general appearance, my driver is a dynamic character, and his whole being almost crackles with energy. I suspect he does everything quickly and competently, and hope that also applies to his driving. As he jinks his way through slowly-moving knots of arriving and departing travellers, I am pleased to learn he speaks excellent English. He says his name is Milen, and tells me the proper Bulgarian way to spell it. He makes up for his lack of height and slight frame with his aura of energy and enthusiasm and has curly black and well-trimmed hair, neat features and very white teeth which he likes to show. Overall, he looks the sort of man who would always see a glass as half-full, and if eyes could twinkle, his certainly would.

We weave through and outpace a final gaggle of exiting passengers and I think how Milen would be a runaway winner in the Gatwick Stakes. Then as we reach the pavement, I see what may be the reason for his haste.

Every airport has minders whose job it is to make sure that drivers either pay to use the car parks or drop their passengers off without actually stopping. A tall woman in grey uniform is showing interest in the shiny people-carrier we are approaching, and I see that, though it bears no insignia, it is standing in the taxi rank. We arrive at the car and a rapid exchange takes place, I don't know what they are saying but imagine it is the same in any language. The woman looks unimpressed and opens her black book. Milen looks crestfallen, then inspiration strikes and he whips out the photograph of me, holds it in front of her face and lets out another machine-gun burst.

The warden looks at the photo and then at me with as much doubt as Milen had indicated earlier, so I smile and turn so that the sun is at my back then lift my chin to tauten the sagging flesh. Eventually, she appears to accept that I am me and also who Milen says I am. With a shrug that shows how unimpressed she is, she looks me up and down, closes her booking book and goes off in search of another victim.

Milen loads my bag into the boot and opens the front passenger door. As I settle in and belt up I ask him what he told the lady. He smiles and twinkles and explains the lady now thinks she has met the famous British film star Oliver Reed. She said she had seen me in *Gladiator* and that I was shorter and not so attractive in real life. He responded that it is marvellous what they can do with cameras nowadays.

As we drive away and join the fray of Sofia traffic, Milen says he knows that the legendary hell-raiser and drinker died of over-indulgence at about the time the photo of me was taken, but the lady with the notebook clearly does not.

На пътя
On The Road

Travel writer Bill Bryson was walking back to his hotel in Sofia when he reflected that Bulgaria was not a country, but a near-death experience. I reckon he was looking at passing traffic when he came up with that one. The capital of Bulgaria is home to more than a million people. Most seem to be on the roads, and all drive madly or badly or both.

The country has a truly shocking record for road traffic accidents and deaths, and I can see why. I have driven in Paris and Rome, Moscow and Madrid and not observed anywhere near this level of capital insanity.

I think it true to say that each country has its own way of driving badly, and that national stereotypes seem particularly apt when it comes to using the road. The British drive thoughtlessly, stupidly or aggressively (sometimes all at the same time), the French selfishly and arrogantly, and the Italians as if they have a hot date to get to.

At this early stage, it seems to me that the Bulgars - or at least those who drive in Sofia - simply don't give a shit, and may actually like having near-death experiences.

They are either deceptively skilful, or really don't care about the outcome of switching lanes without warning and racing through apparently impossible gaps.

The strange thing is that, unlike in other countries (and the UK in particular), nobody seems to mind about being a victim of a manoeuvre which puts their vehicle or life in jeopardy. Perhaps this is because they score so low on the UN World Happiness index and are not fussed about whether they live or die. Or perhaps it is because their vehicles are so old and mangled they are not bothered about notching up another dent or disability. In Paris and other capitals it is not uncommon for wealthy motorists to leave their classy motors at home and use a banger to get around in town. But here, apart from the odd sinister-looking black limo or 4 x 4 with impenetrable windows, all the vehicles look as if they are competing at a stock car derby and getting into practice on the way. I also have evidence that I am not alone in my conclusions.

The official view of the United States Embassy as expressed on its website is that driving in Bulgaria is 'extremely dangerous' and confrontations with the owners of late-model vehicles should be avoided, as they may well be driven by 'armed organized crime figures.'

Not counting those shot by irritated Mafia members, Bulgaria has the highest rate of road deaths in Europe. The average in the EU is 51 per million of the population; in Bulgaria it is 95. The figures speak for themselves, as do the scenes through the windscreen of Milen's Ford Galaxy.

Like those in Moscow, the roads of central Sofia are boulevard-wide and straight; unlike Moscow, they appear to have been recently strafed and bombed. Until now I thought Belgium held the record for rotten driving surfaces, but now I see they are not a patch on this bit of Bulgaria. All around us, cars are swerving wildly to avoid the larger potholes while happily taking on those less than a foot deep. Ahead, I see a tyre is wedged into a miniature crater and remark to Milen that someone has actually lost a wheel. He smiles and says that the tyre is not a casualty, but a marker put there to warn drivers that the hole is too big to drive over unless you are in a tractor or tank.

I nod and shut my eyes as he crosses four lanes by the shortest route and pulls up on what would be an expressway if it were not for the traffic-calming potholes. As soon as we stop, a hand holding a parcel is thrust through the driver's window. Milen exchanges it for a bundle of crumpled notes, casually tosses the package on to the back seat and rejoins the tide of traffic. When he invited me to join him in the front of the Galaxy, I thought he wanted to practice his English or point out the sights of Sofia; now I realise he is not running a taxi company but a bespoke people and parcel delivery service.

So far we have picked up two passengers and three packages and have not reached the outskirts of the capital. This explains why the fare for my fifty mile journey is almost risibly cheap even by Bulgarian standards.

There are three mobile phones on the dashboard, and they ring, squawk or beep constantly. I don't know what the law is about using phones while driving, but observation of other road users suggests that it may be compulsory to eat, smoke, pick your nose or talk to someone not in the car while on the road. Milen manages to use at least one phone at a time while driving and making notes about pick-up points and times. He does this by getting one of the passengers in the seat behind to literally lend a hand and hold a phone to his ear, and at one point even asks me to take the wheel while he turns a page in his notepad. He is, however, a clearly competent and relatively reserved driver, so I try and relax and take in my surroundings.

The airport is ten kilometres east of the city centre, but we are battling our way through the heart of Sofia. Milen says it is so I can see the sights, but I think he also may have more packets and passengers to pick up.

It is certainly worth the delay for me, as I now realise that the capital of Bulgaria is a place of fascinating contrasts. Apart from the dire road surfaces (which in places disprove the old Portuguese adage that grass does not grow on a busy street) the buildings in the outskirts are a strange mixture of ancient, modern and complete crap. In contrast and as if it is a deliberately constructed centrepiece, the heart of the city is filled with a slew of sometimes dramatically opulent buildings. The imposing Saint Sofia Basilica dates back to the 6th-century and was used as a mosque during the Turkish occupation. The Alexander Nevsky cathedral is a multi-tiered and domed and over-the-top wedding cake delight, while the soaring columns of the former Communist Party Headquarters must have been calculated to overawe and keep the People in their place.

Just a mile on, and we are in a jungle of shabby, drab and colourless tenements, some of which, perversely, seem enhanced by the virulently coloured graffiti. The sudden change is like travelling from Knightsbridge to the most deprived parts of Hackney in a trice, or perhaps in a madly-driven Bulgarian cab. There are rubble-strewn and junk-filled gaps between buildings which remind me of bomb damages in east London after WWII, and someone has sprayed *All Coppers Are Bastards* on one of the few remaining walls of a roof, door and windowless shell. In some places whole pavements are missing, and the pedestrians pick their way across bare clay.

In the commercial areas, the most common outlets seem to be shops advertising alcohol for sale 24/7, and casinos with Las Vegas-style names which do not suit their shoddy exteriors. Curiously, many of the shop signs and all the advertisements for the booze outlets are, like the graffiti, in English.

As we reach the outskirts, the buildings get smaller and plainer and less dramatically scruffy. Strangely, the road surfaces are in marginally better condition and I haven't seen a pothole big enough to take a tyre for some time.

Then, as we pull up at a junction I see a sight you do not often encounter in London. A small and elegant-looking pony is toeing the white line as it waits impatiently for the lights to change. It is obviously well-nourished and cared for and is tethered to a low wooden cart with a car wheel and tyre at each corner. The bodywork has outwardly sloping sides but no back or front, and it looks about the right size and shape to carry a coffin.

Holding the reins is a middle-aged man in shirtsleeves and trousers which end at calf height. He has coal-black hair, European features and a natural colouring that is darker than seasoned oak. In the body of the cart sits a small woman. It is hard to tell her age, as her nut-brown face seems prematurely lined. She is wearing a voluminous skirt, a colourful and much-beaded top and the sort of tight-fitting, head-covering bandana affected by ageing American owners of Harley Davidson motorcycles. She seems to sense I am looking at her, and turns her head my way. Her look is incurious, and she does not respond beyond a puzzled frown when I give an embarrassed idiot's smile and wave. She is clearly used to being stared at, but I wonder how many of the lookers acknowledge her so effusively.

The lights change and Milen puts his foot down and we leave the Roma gypsy couple behind. As we head for the hills I wonder what part they play in the life of their capital city, and what they think of it.

~

We are in another world.

I didn't know what to expect of the Balkans, but had some sort of general idea of a series of rocky ridges with snow on the highest peaks.

That's not an altogether inadequate description, but the whole is somehow far more than the sum of its parts. It is all so, well, spectacular.

The Balkan Peninsula covers a number of countries with, in the past, constantly changing borders. The region gets its name from the mountain range almost entirely contained within Bulgaria and which stretches eastwards from the border with Serbia for 560 kilometres to the Black Sea.

The range encompasses many prehistoric cave dwellings - some with wall paintings - and gorges, waterfalls, rock formations and nature parks. The Balkan range is also home to a wide variety of wildlife, including chamois, black squirrels, deer, boar, brown bears and, allegedly, wolves. Simply because it is there, the Balkans range has played a huge part in the history of Bulgaria. It has also affected the transport situation.

It is only fifty miles from the airport to our destination but the drive will take more than two hours. This is not just because of Milen's drop-offs and pick-ups, but because of the undulations of the mountain pass.

When Bulgaria joined the EU in 2007, there were some exciting plans mooted for creating a luxurious ski-holiday destination in the mountains near to where we are heading. *The piece de resistance* was to drive a tunnel through the Balkans from Sofia and thus halve the journey time, but it came to nothing. There were some speculative land grabs with sometimes ludicrous sums paid for what would be key areas in town and countryside, and dark mutterings about corruption in high places.

It is beyond dispute that much money has gone to the wrong pockets as a result of less well-off countries joining the EU. It is estimated that corruption everywhere costs the European Union more than 160 billion Euros every year, and Romania and Bulgaria head the list of allegations and investigations.

But here, even the very air is pure and untainted.

Having left behind the elevated plain on which the capital sits, we are now traversing a wonderland of great pine forests, giant boulders, mountain cascades and streams and glorious flora. The pass takes the form of a switchback road of constant hairpins and other blind corners, and perversely, the driving seems to become increasingly more cavalier as the road becomes more dangerous.

Perhaps the drivers think that because they know what is round the next bend it does not matter if it is a ten tonne Eurolorry on the wrong side of the road. For whatever reasons and despite the perils, the driving is generally careless and occasionally life-threatening.

As I take a tighter grip on the door handle and try to concentrate on the scenery, there is a roar like a fighter jet flying at chimney pot height as a late-model Mercedes rockets by. It is heading straight at a huge truck laden with logs which is labouring up the road towards us. There is no leeway for the lorry driver to take evasive action because of the sheer drop on his side, and we are taking up most of the side of the road which ends in a retaining wall of stone blocks. Milen brakes savagely, as does the driver of the log lorry, and the Mercedes flies through the gap with no more than a coat or two of paint to spare.

The strange thing is that I am the only one swearing at the driver of the black limo, or in the least put out by the incident. The man at the wheel of the truck had not flashed his lights or sounded his horn, though he would hardly have had time. None of the passengers behind me comment or even let out a sigh of relief, and Milen merely picks up speed again and reaches for two of the phones which are calling for his attention. Apparently, this sort and level of near-death experience on the roads is so common that it is not even noteworthy.

~

My heart rate has almost returned to normal when we arrive at a break in the walls of forest and stone and join a queue of cars at a police checkpoint. A couple of blue and white Opels sit in the car park outside a bar, and a group of generously overfed officers are gathered by a temporary road block made of a two rusty tripods supporting a striped barrier like an oversized barber's pole. There is something of a 1960s Cold War spy film about the scene, but they have clearly picked the wrong extras to play the standard ferret-faced and menacing East European border guards. These police men are mostly built for comfort, and their full figures and rumpled uniforms dispel any sense of menace, even allowing for the low-slung gun belts. It is clear that they are not low-slung to aid a fast draw, but to support sizeable paunches. Four of the six officers are leaning against one of the parked police cars as they watch a single colleague manning the barrier. Two are drinking from plastic cups and enjoying a cigarette. The other two are engaged in battle with what look like huge double-decker two-handed sandwiches, though one manages to also hold a cup and cigarette. The ones taking it easy must be on a break, or perhaps the overkill of personnel is another hangover from the communist era policy of full employment and low wages.

I am pleased to see that they have pulled the black limo over, and one of the policemen on the barrier is leaning down and talking to an occupant through a lowered back window. I consider getting out and having a word with the madman and telling the policeman about his driving standards, then think of two good reasons for not so doing.

One is that I can't speak Bulgarian; the other is based on the advice on the US Embassy website. The Mercedes fits the description of the sort of model favoured by organised crime figures. Also, the policeman is not talking to the driver, but someone in the back seat who must be important enough to have a chauffeur. He must also be fatalistic enough to let him drive like a lunatic. I reflect on how the murder rate in Bulgaria is actually below average for the European Union, but this is said to be because the criminals usually concentrate on killing each other and don't bother with civilians.

As we watch, I ask Milen if the policemen will be checking on licences and insurance and the equivalent of MOT certification. He smiles wryly and says it is more likely that they are looking for drugs or guns or illegal immigrants... or are just bored and fancied a break and a chat.

Then the policeman talking to the Mercedes driver straightens up. He does not actually salute, but waves the car on with the sort of unnecessarily theatrical and urgent wave that is given to fire engines, ambulances and cars carrying VIPs.

It is our turn at the makeshift barrier, and as we draw up the policemen looks through the windscreen, smiles and waves us straight through with a gesture almost as over-the-top as the one used on the Mercedes. It is obvious that Milen is a friend or even relative of the officer, but I wonder about the identity of the passenger in the Mercedes with the blacked-out windows. Perhaps he really is a member of the local crime syndicate, a local bigwig, or even a colleague who teaches fellow officers advanced driving techniques.

~

We are heading downhill, and the route seems even steeper and more switchback than the way up.

There is much less forestation here, and we pass the occasional huddle of houses and long, single storey buildings that Milen says are abandoned farm collectives. When the communists came, he adds, they put all the land into common ownership, which in reality meant in the hands of those at the top. The stable-like buildings of breeze blocks and corrugated tin roofs were not built to house animals, but workers.

As we pass through the roadside settlements, I see that many of the houses have a small table set up on the verge. On them are jars in various hues under the proprietorship of usually elderly men or women. They make no sales pitch, and sit with arms crossed or hands in laps, looking straight ahead as if contemplating the past, or what is left of their future. They are very, very still, and I have seen people pretending to be statues on the South Bank of the Thames who are more mobile. As Milen explains, they are hoping that passers-by will stop and buy a jar of honey.

As I know from my research, as well as rose oil and yogurt, this part of Europe is famed for its honey. It has always been a desirable and versatile natural product, and in Roman times was used to pay taxes. In Ancient Greece, women would dip their finger in honey before a wedding to ensure their married life would be sweet. Bulgaria is said to be an ideal location for the production of the finest honey because of its climate and diversity of plant life. It is known here as liquid gold because of its taste, medicinal properties and export value. It is also a vital cottage industry. I ask Milen if all these houses will have hives in the garden, and he smiles and says this area is not known to be popular with bees. It is in fact said that some of the villagers buy honey in the supermarket then re-jar it to appeal to passing tourists.

~

I am the sole passenger in Milen's mini-bus, and we have arrived in Montana.

Care should be taken not to confuse the province of Montana in Bulgaria with the state in the United States of America. They are similar in some respects, but much different in others.

The American Montana is in the western region of the USA, and its name derives from the Spanish for 'mountain'. The average income of the million people who live there is high and it is part of the Rocky Mountain range.

Bulgaria's Montana is also in the west and is one of 28 provinces. The biggest town bears the same name, which comes from the Latin for 'mountain'. The population of the province is around 148,000 and falling, and is home to the country's largest concentration of Roma gypsies. Montana is also the poorest province in Bulgaria.

~

The mountain roads with their heart-stopping hairpin bends are behind us, and we are traversing a great plain. The dual carriageway runs straight and true and wide and potholes are rare. Perhaps, in a perverse Bulgarian sort of way, this is why the standard of driving seems much less suicidal here.

I see a sign showing a badge with the word 'vignette' beneath it in non-Cyrillic script, and Milen says it concerns the Bulgarian equivalent of road tax. To drive on a properly maintained route like this one, drivers must pay for and display a badge. There is no charge to anyone to use country roads and lanes, and a standing joke is that the government should technically have to pay drivers to risk their lives and vehicles on them.

A river runs on one side and what looks like a single-track railway line on the other. Occasionally we pass what are either car breaker's yards or perhaps even collection points for wreckage from accidents. At one there are dozens of bumpers of different designs and colours lined up facing the road, and most bear evidence of having hit something rather hard. Perhaps, given the driving standards, car owners like to buy pre-stressed and damaged bumpers to save doing it themselves.

Now and then we pass shanty-like buildings made of odd bits of wood and metal. They all have a parcel of cultivated land alongside or behind them, so may be large garden sheds or even small homes. Outside one, a figure is breaking new ground with what looks like an expensive Rotavator. He stops as we pass, sees me watching and takes off his flat cap and waves it.

Beyond the small plots of land, the plain stretches for miles, unbroken by fences or hedges and apparently growing only shrubs and weeds. Milen sees me frowning at such a waste of space and says that this part of Bulgaria was once a thriving agricultural hub. Since the Communists arrived and departed, the fields have never returned to what they were.

The Galaxy slows as Milen indicates left and prepares to leave the main road. He studies his offside wing mirror diligently, and explains that some drivers like to overtake just as the car in front is about to cross their path.

We make it in spite of a game attempt to ram us by what looks like a World War II Russian ambulance, and cross the bridge on the wrong side to avoid a truly impressive hole through which the river can be seen. It is shallow and stony and fast-running, and Milen says it is a good place to pan for gold. I look at him to see if he is joking, but he says there is much gold in the area and he has a friend who will take me on a day's prospecting if I would like. He adds that many Bulgarians are treasure hunters and self-confessed looters, and panning for gold or using metal detectors to find ancient booty is almost a national sport.

We clatter over the bridge and pick our way past some interestingly-shaped potholes and miniature crevasses. On either side of the road, the fields lie uncultivated, with some sparsely occupied by horses and donkeys and the odd huddle of sheep and goats. The horses and donkeys are unattended, but wherever there are sheep and goats, there is someone on watch. I don't know if they are protecting their charges from wolves or rustlers or it is just a part of the rhythm of their lives, but the sitting or standing figures are as still and within themselves as the honey-sellers in the mountains

Ahead is a long commercial building, and a rank smell of decay wafts into the car. Milen sees my face and says it is a bad day at the local meat processing factory. He grimaces, puts his foot down and we rapidly leave the drab buildings and odour behind.

~

If this is our destination, I am not impressed. I don't know exactly what I expected of a Bulgarian mountain village, but this one could not be less quaint.

We are still at the level of the plain, and any view of higher ground is obstructed by the lines of drab houses on either side of the narrow road. With their mostly colourless and unadorned box-like appearance they could be properties on a giant Monopoly board. All are uniform in shape and look as if they were made to exactly the same specification. Each is a cube of much-weathered brick of two storeys and with rusty-railed external stone steps leading to the upper level. Some are rendered, while some have severely distressed brick or blocks on show, and their general condition varies greatly. A surprising number are abandoned, with gaping holes where the windows would have been. Many roofs have collapsed or may even have been looted for their components. Nearly all are in a pretty poor condition, but the occupied properties generally have well-kept gardens. The overall impression is of the fecundity of nature. Beyond high rusty wire fencing and the sort of gates you would expect to see on a poorly-maintained tennis court, tall wooden frameworks are festooned with vines and surprisingly plumptious bunches of grapes, and crowded vegetable plots and fruit trees and bushes are the colour of summer.

Next to most of the cubist houses is a much older building, usually close to or totally in ruin. Milen explains that the new houses were built in the 1950's as part of a communist drive to re-house villagers in something more up-to-date than mud-walled hovels. The new homes had and still have no bathrooms or kitchens, and the toilets are no more than holes in the ground, but all have electricity and running water. The old cottages are used for storage and animals, or in some cases by the owners who prefer to live in the house where they were born.

There are no cars on show, but parked on the roadside verges is the occasional truck which looks of the same vintage as the communist-era homes. A little further along, we pass a lay-by which is filled with the corpses of cars, lorries and coaches. I note from the make and model and faded signage that one would have been used to take British workers on daytrips to the seaside at about the same time as the houses here were being built. I don't know how it got here, but I can already see that Bulgarians don't like to waste anything.

Now we are approaching the centre of the village, where stands a church of a similar size and shape to a Nissen hut, and made of the same sort of materials as the temporary WW11 shelters. Its function is identified by a green-painted wooden cross fixed to the ridge on its corrugated-iron roof.

There are signs of life in the village, and outside most of the houses we pass sit elderly women - and they are all women. Some are alone, others in groups of two or three. They have no tables with goods for sale, so I assume they are just watching the world go by. The road is clearly so little-used that a car must be a bit of a talking point, and all the ladies wave or at least nod as we pass.

We splash and clatter across a ford and on to a small patch of greenery on which stands an apparently newly-erected wooden shelter. It has no doors or windows, and fixed to the outside is a large map. Inside at a table, four ladies sit. They are mostly of middle-age and are talking animatedly as they help each other to drinks from giant plastic bottles and food from plates of what look like delicate fancy cakes. They lift their glasses in salute as we pass, and Milen explains that the shelter was built with the help of a Euro grant to provide visiting hikers with somewhere to rest and study the layout of the surrounding. As there have been no hikers passing this way since it was built, some of the younger women have taken the hut over as a place to meet and dine. I lift an arm and doff my straw hat to the village luncheon club, and ask Milen if we have reached our destination.

He smiles and says no. We are heading for Krasiva, which is the upper village. This is Komerinski, the lower village. The two villages have the same sort of buildings and average age of resident, but are very different. The people of Komerinski have the river and the meat factory, which is a plus or minus depending on which way the wind is blowing. But the people of Krasiva have what is locally held to be the best view in the Balkans.

~

This is more like it.

The road begins to wind and rise steeply immediately beyond Komerinski, and there is already a feeling of wild openness. Then, I instinctively duck as a shadow passes over the windscreen and a pterodactyl comes in to land on a monstrous nest sitting on top of a telegraph pole. It's the first time I've seen a stork this close up, and Milen says there is a pair in the giant nest. The father has just returned with food for his mate, and she is waiting for the birth of her brood.

I crane my neck to watch them until we take a bend and start to climb steeply, then suddenly I see what all the fuss is about.

We have arrived on the rim of a great bowl of a valley, which is very, very green. In the not-so-far distance, a jagged line of mountains meets the clouds. In between the mountains and the valley is a vast forest. Below us, red-roofed doll's houses are scattered carelessly alongside the river we crossed earlier. Milen tells me that the rainbow-coloured boxes outside some of the houses are bee hives. They are miniature cubist versions of the Communist houses, but painted in a spectrum of bright colours. Perhaps, I think, the explosion of colour is a reaction against the drab conformity of the era.

A contented clutch of cows are grazing alongside the river, and though they are afar, I can hear their bells through the open window. On the slopes on the higher side of the road, thousands of staked grape vines in rigidly straight lines take the eye up to more dense woodland. Above all this, an eagle wheels majestically across the great blue bowl of cloudless sky.

Whatever I was expecting, this panorama certainly tops it. In most other places, people would fight to live somewhere like this. Here, the village of Krasiva is dying, and in the midst of such natural splendour it must be wondering why.

~

We have a 9th-century monk and his brother to thank for the Cyrillic alphabet. It is a mixture of Greek and ancient church scripts which was clearly devised to perplex and confuse foreign travellers for all time. The roadside sign announces that we are entering КРАСИВА, but someone has thoughtfully written the non-Cyrillic version beneath.

Though in an infinitely better setting, the houses on either side of the road on the outskirts seem in no better fettle than those in the lower village. Regardless of condition, all must have spectacular views, though how much of a compensation this is to those who live in them I cannot know. I breathe deeply, and the air is sweet and flavoured by the roadside plants and wildflowers. At this height the air must be pure, and we are the only vehicle bringing pollution to Krasiva.

We stop for a tinkling bevy of nanny-goats to cross the road, and an androgynous figure swathed in many layers of clothing lifts a staff in acknowledgement. We drive slowly on and another villager comes into view. The lady is clearly very old and stick-thin, but defiantly upright. Over baggy harem-style trousers, she is wearing a heavily-patterned, loose and knee-length top with narrow sleeves and no collar. On her head is a bandanna-style headscarf as worn by the Roma woman we saw in Sofia. This lady's face is lined and weathered, but the high cheekbones and firm chin and jawline lend her face an air of ageless dignity. She walks slowly and deliberately, and has a bag of some sort of embroidered material hanging from one shoulder. Like a skier on a hard-going level surface, she is using two sticks to help make her way. Milen touches his forehead in greeting and she nods almost regally as she continues what must be her painful way towards an unusual house on the high side of the road. It is a three-storey building, but has no frames in the windows on the top floor. Milen says she was born in the mud-walled cottage alongside, and has never left the village. It was a custom in the old days to start with a single-storey house, and add a floor for each new generation. This lady has no grandchildren, so the top floor was never finished. She was married for many years but her husband died some years ago. Most days she walks to the shop in the village square. She could have her groceries dropped off by a neighbour, but Milen thinks she prefers to walk to show her independence and that she can still make the mile-long journey.

~

It would not take Sherlock Holmes to deduce that we have reached our destination.
Bought and restored to accommodate visitors to the Moore's domain, the Guest House is so pristine it looks more Home Counties than Balkan village.

There are no hanging baskets or brightly painted wagon wheels adorning the walls of the solid, red-brick house; what makes it stand out is simply that there is nothing wrong with it. The roof tiles are all accounted for and in their proper places, and the zinc guttering and downpipes glister in the noon-day sun.

On nearby properties, the windows are often in rotting state and most are barren of curtains. Here, they are gleaming white and graced with classy Venetian blinds. Most markedly, there is no line of rusty fencing or heaps of junk in the yard which makes the neighbouring properties resemble the dwelling of a scrap-metal merchant who likes to take his work home with him.

Lying beyond a severely pruned line of plane trees, my home for the summer months sprouts from the slope of the valley. It actually looks as if it could ski down to the distant depths if it were not so well planted. Its passage would anyway be blocked by an ancient cottage, which I know the owners intend to become an artists and artisans workshop. It too has a new roof.

I get out of the Galaxy and nearly step on a dead dog. Eventually, it opens an eye, regards me and the car unconcernedly and goes back to sleep. It is of medium size and with a heavy black coat and of indeterminate race; in general, it is in a better condition than the house next door, outside of which it lies and to which it presumably belongs.

I stretch my arms and savour the sharp, clean air; the dog opens the other eye and looks even more unimpressed before returning to its guard duty. Milen joins me at the roadside, hands me my case and the key to the house and tells me the bill. I am so embarrassed by the piffling amount for ferrying me more than fifty miles that I give him a tip which is bigger than the fare. He looks more surprised than gratified and a shadow passes across his face; then he twinkles again, shakes my hand and is gone in a shower of dust and detritus.

Note to self: Remember where you are and beware of being patronising even if with good intent. I don't think for a moment that Milen was offended by my monster tip, but I must have been reminding him how comparatively wealthy most foreign visitors are, and how hard he has to work to make a living.

I watch the car race off down the narrow lane, then look around and realise what else is so different about this village. Apart from no cars or signs of life, there is not a single television aerial or satellite dish. Coming as I do from one of Britain's most densely occupied cities it is an almost unnerving sight, and makes it seem as if I had travelled in time as well as space.

I pick my way down the neatly grassed slope, then up the concrete steps to the first floor entry. On the landing, a severely dilapidated cooking range stands against the ornamental railings. I know that this would once have been the place where food was prepared and cooked, and it is ironic to think that, tarted up, the old stove would probably sell in a We-Saw-You-Coming boutique in London for more than the house cost to build.

Inside, the cool hallway leads on to three large, high-ceilinged rooms. The one facing the road has become a well-equipped kitchen, with a shower room and toilet alongside. Another door leads to the bedroom, which has a double aspect. One window looks out to the road and dormant dog; the other frames what is an almost breathtaking view. It is so impossibly spectacular that it reminds me of one of those giant friezes of stunning panoramas pasted on sitting-room walls in the 1970s. But I am looking at the real thing. In the foreground is the river and valley bed, then the forest, and beyond that the western end of the Balkans. Looking down from the highest part of the range is the mighty King Kom.

At 2016 metres, Kom comfortably tops its nearest rival, and even at this time of year the peak is snow-covered. There is a hiking trail of 700 kilometres along the Stara Planina range, and all the peaks above 2000 metres are within its length. To the proud citizens of the nearest town, it is known as *Golyam* (Big) Kom, and it has *Streden* (Middle) and *Malak* (Small) brothers. The distinguished Bulgar writer Ivan Vazov was moved to write a poem in salute to Kom, and part of it is on a plaque at the peak. Kom's fame has travelled far, and there is a glacier named for it in Antarctica. To seasoned mountaineers, Kom is known merely as a 'walk-up' and I mean to try to climb it before I leave. If I make it, I shall certainly not refer to it so dismissively when telling the tale of my epic battle with the mighty and deadly mountain peak.

~

My bag is unpacked and socks and tee-shirts and (at my wife's insistence) far too many pairs of underpants have been stowed away.

They are in a chest of drawers which looks as if it would be more at home in a traditional gypsy caravan. The combination of Damien Hirst-style dots and runic symbols in very bright colours is not to my taste, but you can see that Sally Moore is a very skilled wielder of a brush. The theme is continued with other suitable furniture, and Sally and her husband are obviously also skilled at sniffing out the sort of unusual period pieces which would be snapped up for big money in a trendy London shop or market. There is no central heating or boring electric or gas fires in the house, but each room is dominated by huge and hugely ornate stoves. Like Victorian versions of something from a *Transformers* movie, they squat well away from walls, connected with very large flue pipes. At first I think that having the stoves so distant from the walls is a silly idea, then realise that, doing it this way means the heat from the flues will stay in the room.

After unpacking, I explore the rest of the house and can see that considerable thought and work has gone into transforming the communist cube on the inside.

At ground level are three rooms in the process of being updated, and a new internal staircase leads up to the first floor and then on to the attic. Someone has done a splendid job of leaving the old beams and rafters in place while installing two dormer windows looking out over the valley. One is inaccessible because of a lack of flooring; the other gives on to a slab of projecting concrete which has yet to be railed. Now, I am sitting on the nascent balcony and drinking coffee as I take in the even more breathtaking view my elevated position affords.

Despite or perhaps because of the view, I'm thinking of how I came to be in this place to write a magazine article about the owners of this house and their plan to save Krasiva from its continuing decline and apparently inevitable death. Looking at the panorama and knowing the story of how the owners of this property came to be here, it seems to me that fate and circumstance can sometimes rule or at least interfere with our lives and their outcome.

Sally and Richard Moore first came to Bulgaria after the

tragic death of their son Sam. Their plan is to create an artistic community while at the same time helping save Krasiva from its otherwise inevitable decline and death.

Their highly unusual and, some would say eccentric scheme involves buying up local properties, restoring them and putting them up for sale to a very specialist market. The proposition is to appeal to people who would like the idea of having an extraordinarily cheap bolthole in the Balkans in which to give full vent to their creative juices.

Eventually and if all goes to plan, a thriving arts and crafts community will replace the original villagers as they pass on to their reward. The really, really unusual aspect of the project is that Sally and Richard will only sell to the right sort of prospective buyer, and the whole scheme is to be non-profit making, which should not be hard.

This most altruistic of schemes may sound completely crackers and probably is. Having met them on a dozen occasions, I am convinced that the Moores are genuine and almost completely non-materialistic. They know that people from nearby towns will not want to move to the countryside no matter how well the houses of Krasiva are restored. As all the statistics prove, the migration by young, middle-aged and even elderly Bulgarians to urban surroundings and other countries is clearly irreversible.

So, former art teacher Sally and her husband are on a mission to re-populate the village with the sort of people who would be attracted to the idea of living in a remote part of the glorious Balkans whilst they carry out their creative projects.

From what I have seen so far, the Moores are sincere in their aims. But I also think that they just love buying houses and doing them up. This would be an impossibly expensive hobby in the United Kingdom, but achievable in a country where you can buy a dilapidated property for the cost of a dodgy second-hand car in Britain.

So, more and more empty houses in the village will be bought, restored and then, if all goes to plan, sold on to artists and writers and artisans - or anyone with an interest in art and nature. The idea, in brief, is for a sort of laid-back arts and crafts movement set in the sylvan surroundings of the Balkans.

But I think it is more than that.

Sally and Richard believe that new life can be breathed into Krasiva, while helping the aged population and establishing a monument to their son.

I love the idea of an artistic collective living and working alongside the locals in a remote Bulgarian village, but fear the couple may be being more than a little unrealistic; for sure, they are at the upper end of the eccentricity scale.

~

It is not every home that boasts a Roman sarcophagus in the shed.

The concrete coffin was found while the earth floor of the old cottage was being dug up to make head height for any authors or craftspeople over the height of five feet who might want to work there. A spade hit something solid and exposed what the diggers took to be an old stone water-butt. But the chances are that it is a child's casket, dating back to the first Roman occupation.

As I stand and think about who it would have been made for and how he or she died, I hear a shout and walk out into the sunshine. The garden of the guesthouse slopes down to a hedge of bramble and saplings, and through it a sheep is struggling. It is followed by another, then a donkey, then the shouter. He sees me watching and walks up the slope, using his staff to help navigate between tussocks of couch grass and piles of animal droppings.

The man is of average height, and strongly-made. He is apparently in late middle age, and a leading contender for my ongoing Foreign Countryman (or Woman) Most Luxuriant Moustache competition.

Despite the warmth of the day, he is wearing an overcoat belted with string, and a fedora hat which looks even more weathered than his face. Puffing slightly, he arrives at my side, raises the staff and gives me a gummy smile before letting out a burst of Bulgarian which either means 'Welcome to Krasiva' or 'What the fuck do you think you're doing here?'

I do the usual idiot smile and placatory nod employed by strangers in a foreign land who do not speak the language. As the donkey ambles over and investigates the crutch of my shorts to see if it contains anything edible, its owner tries another burst and then waits expectantly. When I give him another sickly, apologetic smile, he shrugs, returns the smile and goes back to his shepherding duties. He is probably wondering how a man can reach my age and not be able to speak Bulgarian, and who the thickie intruder is. As he settles down in the garden, I return to the house to find my Bulgarian phrase book. These sorts of publications can be helpful for general enquiries, but I doubt there is a post office or public toilet in the vicinity I shall need to ask the way to.

Среща на президента
Meeting the President

The Moores live literally off the beaten track in a cottage which pre-dates the Guest House by a couple of centuries.

To use estate agent speak, it lies in an undisturbed location with stunning views, and yet close to the heart of the village and its facilities. In Bulgarian terms, this means it is half-way down a dead-end dirt track off the lane which leads to the square and the sometimes-open village shop. It certainly has views which would challenge the most hyperbolic of estate agents' phrase books. It would also be true to say that many of the surrounding properties have been undisturbed by improvement or maintenance work since they were built.

The small, beamed, red brick and tiled cottage stands at the top of a hillock overlooking the valley. It is clear from the outside that my hosts' home has been carefully and even artfully restored, while most of the neighbouring properties have been left to mature naturally. Others look as if they have been deliberately distressed. In extreme cases all that remains of some former dwellings is a wall or two of time-smoothed clay, suggesting a giant sandcastle after the tide has come in.

As to the occupants of the neighbouring homes, so far I have seen and met more animals than people. Small gangs of chickens roam and peck bossily in no danger from traffic or other predators. Dogs lie in the sun or look wistfully through wire fencing, and goats and sheep contest mostly amicably for grazing rights. In the near distance, a donkey brays, a dog barks plaintively and one of my fellow dinner guests shouts an obvious admonition. Although his voice is stern, it is in the mock-angry tone of a fond parent.

Sitting across the table on the terrace overlooking the village, valley and the mountains is my new friend Elenko. He is still wearing the moustache, but not the hat or overcoat. I have already learned that he lives in one of the more well-maintained cottages along the track, and some of the livestock there belongs to him. As well as the sheep and Chiro the donkey, he has a handful of hens, a cat named Choco and a dog called Bingo - which is the name of a popular washing powder.

I now know that Elenko is approaching seventy and - apart from his menagerie - lives alone. Sally says he has a wife and son in town, but they only visit when an animal needs to be slaughtered. The two sheep I met today looked as elderly and potentially inedible as their owner, so will probably live out their natural life spans unless his wife comes to call in search of some very mature mutton.

What Elenko did before retirement is not clear, but nowadays he looks after his vegetable patch, makes hay for the winter while the sun shines - which is very often - and, like most of the other villagers, walks miles every day to get free summer food for his animals.

The situation regarding land ownership can be complex since the departure of the communist regime, but villagers have their own regular and agreed grazing areas and rights. Some places are communal, some - like the

Guest House garden - are private but belong to people who are happy to have grass and weeds trimmed, and some are secret.

From the yappy evidence, it is a rare house in Krasiva without a dog, and many of the villagers keep or raise other animals for food, a small income, or, like Elenko, just for company. The preponderance of donkeys is explained by the wooden mini-carts standing outside houses where cars would be parked in more prosperous villages.

Part of Elenko's day is spent caring for the Moore's gardens, and this part of Bulgaria is clearly the most fertile of places. Most houses have a lemon bush or tree by the door and a great swathe of grape vines above and around them, and figs, walnut, apple, pear, peach, plum, quince, mulberry and nectarine trees jostle for space with vegetable plots and herb gardens.

I have already learned a little about Bulgaria and life in the countryside here, because Sally takes a great interest in the village and local matters, and Richard in the past of the area and the country. They speak some Bulgarian, but our main interpreter, local historian and potential celebrity lookalike has joined us for dinner.

Ivalin Dimitrov is a remarkable man in a number of ways. He speaks excellent English, but with a Slavic accent so pronounced it sounds like a parody. In fact, it is almost uncannily like the Russian meerkat in the currently popular television advertisement for a comparison website.

Ivalin's appearance is also interesting and unusual. He is wiry in build and does not appear to carry an ounce of surplus fat. Facially, he has slightly protruding eyes, a pointed nose, high and sharp cheekbones, full lips and short thinning hair. Overall, his face seems strangely familiar. Then, as he leans forward to strike the table to emphasise a point, I realise of whom he reminds me. Back in the UK I am sure he could make a good living as a lookalike for Vladimir Putin, the president of the Russian Federation.

I know that Ivalin is as close as it comes to an entrepreneur in the area, as he owns a number of commercial raspberry and strawberry fields somewhere in the valley. He is also a locally renowned mountaineer and is said to climb Kom regularly just to keep his hand in. He is clearly proud that three generations of his family have lived in Krasiva, which makes its decline a keener sorrow. His father, he explains in his precise and almost addictive meerkat voice, was named Dimitar, so he is Dimitrov. Had he been a girl his name would have been Dimitrova. He is a true Bulgarian, and can trace his lineage back to the birth of the country in the 7th-century. From his father and grandparents, he knows the cost of communism. Before 1945, he says, his village was a vibrant, happy place with a growing number of young families.

Now the communists have gone, but so has the future of Krasiva.

~

It is perhaps a little-known fact that Bulgaria is a wine producer of world class, making 200,000 tonnes a year. I hope it is better than Elenko's home brew. He has, as is traditional in the Bulgarian countryside, come with his own contribution to the meal. As I have seen, few occupied houses in the village are without their own grapevines. Outside the village, the slopes bristle with soldierly lines of vine-bearing stakes.

Despite this abundance, Ivalin says there is no organised group to make and market local wine as there is in France or Italy. The villagers use a common press and then make their own. It is a custom to add lemonade before bottling, and I think it may be to make it drinkable.

The result is a sort of sweet and yet sour rosé, as if the

Spanish used pink instead of red wine to make *sangria*.

There is another product of the grape to which I have been introduced this evening. It is not unpleasant in taste, but that is because it is tasteless as well as colourless. Every country has its own firewater, usually made from fruit. In Bulgaria it is called *Rakia*. Plum, cherry, apricot, peach or quince can be used in the process, but grape is the fruit of choice here. It is a truly local beverage; drinking 'rakinja' (the ancient name) is mentioned on a shard of 14th-century pottery found in the Balkans. The average alcohol content is around fifty percent, but some are claimed to hit the 90 percent mark. The sample I tried this evening seemed to be neat alcohol, and I reckon could be used to swab wounds and start tractors. It could also be the reason that Elenko has no top teeth.

~

The evening wears on in an enjoyably woozy way.

Dusk is taking its time settling on the valley, and the cooling air is suffused with the smells of the countryside. I am in good company and even Elenko's wine is tasting better.

Sally has organised a traditional meal, and the two Bulgarian guests have brought their contributions. Ivalin's is a creamy dish of mushrooms from the forest surrounding the base of Kom. He has also brought a bottle of strawberry-flavoured *Rakia*. The combination of sweet fruitiness and what rocket fuel must taste like is interesting. I have begun to see strange shapes forming in the darkness beyond the pool of light spreading from the table lamp; this may be because the fungi is hallucinogenic, or that the *Rakia* is taking effect.

In the Bulgarian manner we help ourselves from the pots and dishes crowding the table. Sharing the food this way makes the event less formal and more friendly, which is probably why the custom came about.

As we eat and drink with little regard to western European table manners, Ivalin explains how Krasiva has become what it is.

Before the arrival of communism, there were ten thousand sheep, a thousand beef cattle and hundreds of pigs sharing the vast swathes of pastureland surrounding the village. In a true interpretation of commune-ism, the villagers shared 300 hectares (800 acres) of land dedicated to crops. Then the communists took charge, and the village was doomed. All animals and land became part of what was called a co-operative. The new masters said it meant that the fields and animals now belonged to everyone, and all would have an equal share. In reality and just as in the bad old days, the people lost what little they had, did all the work and the privileged reaped most of the benefits.

Now, Krasiva is a dying echo of its past. There are still more than a hundred homes, but little more than half of them are occupied. The occupants are mostly over seventy, and it has been decades since a child's cry had been heard in the valley. All the young people have gone to work in nearby towns or far-away countries, and like those left behind, the village is dying.

Poverty is a daily reality, with the state pension varying between one to two hundred Euros a month. Funded by the municipality, the store is limited in goods and hours of opening, and, though the Bulgarian flag still flies over the village hall, it has lain unused for years.

Most people, Ivalin said, would think it would be better to re-populate Krasiva with young Bulgarians, but that would require a return to communist diktat and probably a barbed wire enclosure around the village to keep the new residents from escaping. The simple fact is that, apart from those already here, nobody wants to live in Krasiva. And this despite the serene and beautiful environment and homes for sale at prices which are ludicrously low even by Bulgarian standards.

This was why he and other villagers had welcomed Sally and her project to attract foreign buyers. In many other countries, outsiders buying homes and putting up the prices beyond the purse of young people are resented. Here, with no young people wanting to own a home or live in Krasiva, foreigners would be far more welcome than the communists ever were. Particularly he adds, with a Gollum-like widening of his round eyes, foreigners from the United Kingdom. We have taken so many of the country's youngsters, he concludes, old British people with lots of money would seem a fair exchange.

~

One of the leading publishers of international guidebooks advises visitors to Bulgaria not to go out at night when in the countryside. This is not for fear of gangs of roving brigands or wild beasts, but of falling foul of potholes.

I can see what they mean, and my swaying, *Rakia*-induced gait is actually proving helpful. I am on automatic pilot, and my zig-zag course is threading me in between fissures and small craters like a lucky drunk in a mine field.

I am also helped by the bizarre fact that the winding, holey road lined with dark-windowed houses is actually lit by a line of lampposts.

As with the cubist houses, this apparent anomaly is another reminder of communist era times. The lights were installed after the replacement houses were built and another oddity is that, unlike in the average UK town, they all work. Apart from the contrast with the state of the roads and houses, the peculiarity is even more pronounced when you consider that the average rates or council tax levied in Krasiva is the equivalent of between one and four pounds a year.

I said goodbye to Elenko, Choco and Bingo and Chiro the donkey at his front gate after declining his offer of a nightcap. Richard says he has been inside Elenko's home, but Sally has not been invited. It is, he tactfully says, similar inside to outside. The facilities are basic, with a bed, table and chair, a wood-fuelled cooking range and a Heath-Robinson type device which heats water for a shower. Nothing much would have changed inside the centuries-old cottage with the exception of a television set. As Richard observed it is strange to think that, in spite of being physically sheltered from it, Elenko could see the excesses of modern civilisation in the form of episodes of *Sex and the City* dubbed in Bulgarian.

With the confidence of the inebriated, I stride down the slope and past the steps of the main house and into the old cottage. There, I pat my breast pocket for the packet of cigarettes which will never be there, then, after asking respectful permission of the last occupant, sit on the edge of the stone coffin. Remnants of the old door stand against a wall, and the frame makes a portrait few artists could equal. The jagged ridges of the beginning of the Balkan chain stand proud against the star-filled sky, and it looks as if Kom is reaching up to touch the heel of Orion the Hunter.

It has been a long and absorbing first day in Bulgaria. It is of course too soon to come to any sensible or sober judgement, but I think it would be no punishment to live in this lonely, remarkable and very beautiful place.

Ядене и пиене
Eating and drinking

There is no minimum age at which drinking alcohol is permissible in Bulgaria, though you have to be eighteen to buy any. Ninety-six percent of the beer consumed in the country is made in the thirteen major breweries. When last measured, the consumption rate was 73 litres of beer per head. That modest figure of about three pints a week does not, of course, take account of the very young or old, or abstainers - or those who make and drink their own ale. Cider is becoming a popular drink since introduced by one of the foreign-owned breweries, but off-sales still outdo drinks bought on licensed premises. This reflects the Bulgarian fondness for drinking and eating with friends at home.

As the fifth-largest wine producer in the world, Bulgaria makes some very palatable wines including Cabernet Sauvignon, Merlot and Chardonnay. The country also makes its own whisky and vodka, usually stronger than foreign visitors (except from Russia) are used to.

There are other particularly Bulgarian alcoholic favourites. These include the anise-based *Mastika*. The ouzo-like liquor is sometimes injected into a melon or made into a cocktail with the spearmint-based *Menta*. In this form it is known as The Cloud.

For non-drinkers there's creamy, chilled yogurt, mineral water, elderberry juice and the (to me) undrinkable Turkish-style coffee. Then there's *boza*, a weird breakfast favourite with Oriental origins. It is made by boiling wheat, rye and millet and adding lots of sugar. It is slightly alcoholic, which may explain its popularity as a pick-me-up or hangover cure.

Finally, there's a strange reminder of communist rule which has been likened to Scotland's Irn-Bru. Etar is named after a river in northern Bulgaria which is said to be about the same rust-brown colour. Etar is entirely artificial, and still produced by small companies for older people who liked the flavour as well as the system of communism.

~

Any cuisine reflects the country's geographical location in the form of available and easily-grown or caught products. History also plays its part, with dishes and eating habits introduced by generally unwanted visitors. In common with other Balkan countries, Bulgaria shares or has its own versions of Russian, Greek, Turkish and Middle Eastern dishes and diets. Bulgarians also like big servings of all the things we have been told not to eat much of. Bread comes in loaf-sized portions at many restaurants and salt is used with abandon, including on and in some puddings. Meat is predominantly pork and comes in the form of burgers or kebabs or very good, spicy sausages.

At table, family and guests are expected to help themselves from the serving dishes, and foreign visitors are often intrigued by the time lag between the food arriving and the meal beginning. Food grows cold while the hosts chat or serve drinks, and many Bulgarians like to smoke before as well as during and after a meal. My Bulgar friends are still surprised by the way I get stuck in and by what they see as the odd English predilection for eating food while it is still hot.

All the recipes that follow are local or regional variation of national favourites. They were given me by my hosts, the villagers of Krasiva, or various representatives of the Ministry of Tourism. As with the chapter headings, I have added the Cyrillic version of their names just for fun.

шопска салата
Shopska Salata
(shopska salad)

Most countries have a well-known national dish, even if it is not always what foreigners think it is. We Brits are supposed to live on roast beef and fish and chips, though the most popular item on the menu for the United Kingdom nowadays is Tandoori Chicken. Italy is forever associated with pasta, although it is said 13th-century explorer Marco Polo nicked the idea from the Chinese. Some dishes are even named for the country with which they are associated, and Hungary has its goulash as Ireland has its stew.

In Bulgaria, I think it not unfair to say that the national dish is a salad topped with grated cheese. The creation of *Shopska Salata* is credited to the Shopi people of the Sofia region; you will be offered it at just about every restaurant in Bulgaria at any time of year, day or night. As with Cornish pasties, arguments and even violence may occur when the precise ingredients are discussed, but I am told that a proper, family-sized purist's *Shopska* salad should be structured thus:

Ingredients

Four chopped tomatoes
One cucumber, chopped but unpeeled
Two red peppers, seeded and roasted and chopped
Two raw green peppers, chopped
One large yellow onion, chopped
Four smaller green (spring) onions, sliced
Two tablespoons of fresh chopped parsley
Half a cup of sunflower oil
Quarter cup of wine vinegar

Salt and black pepper
Half a cup of crumbled (*not* grated) sirene* cheese

Method

1. Mix the tomatoes and vegetables in a bowl
2. Combine the oil and vinegar and seasoning and toss the salad in it
3. Serve on chilled plates with a topping of the crumbled cheese

Unless I have been looking at the wrong dictionaries, there is no Bulgarian word for cheese. 'Sirene' may be used generally, but specifically refers to a brined, crumbly cheese made from cow or goat or sheep's milk. It is found throughout south-eastern Europe, and as far afield as Israel. The Greeks call it feta, and some of my Bulgarian friends claim that, along with kebabs and yogurt, the idea and recipe originated in their country.

There is another sort of cheese which is called kashkavel and is popular in Bulgaria and surrounding countries. It is semi-hard, yellow and left to mature for six months before it is considered fit to eat. It is said to be called 'the cheddar of the Balkans', but certainly only by those who have never tasted good, proper cheddar. I think it would be put to best use for soling shoes, but it can be rendered almost tasty by using it as an ingredient for all sorts of dishes. This one is universally popular. As the Scots like to deep-fry Mars bars, Bulgarians are very partial to chunks of their national cheese breaded or battered (or both) and fried:

Фасади кашкавал

Kashkavel Pane
(breaded cheese)

Ingredients

Some suitable oil
Some all-purpose flour
500g of kashkavel cheese (provolone, fontina or halloumi
will do equally well)
Three beaten eggs
Two cups of breadcrumbs
Some parsley for garnish

Method

4. Heat three inches of oil in a heavy pan
5. Cut the cheese into half-inch-thick slices
6. Dredge the slices in the flour, then the eggs, then
   the breadcrumbs
7. Fry in batches till golden brown, and drain on
   kitchen roll

Elenko's contribution to our meal was a peculiar mix of dried nettles, wild spinach, onion, green peppers and beaten eggs. In fact, it looked and tasted a right mish-mash, and that is exactly what it is called in Bulgaria. I have not yet discovered if we got our slang term for any messy concoction from them, or they from us. Similar dishes exist in neighbouring and Middle Eastern and Mediterranean countries, and the point is that the recipes vary depending on available foodstuffs and time of year. It might take the form of an omelette like a Spanish *frittata*, or be cooked in a pot in the oven with the eggs added at the end of the process and remaining whole. In the UK the dish has given its name to anything we Brits consider a mix-up, or even a bit of a dog's breakfast.

Elenкоаs мешаніна
Elenkoas miesanina
(Elenko's mish-mash)

Ingredients

Two pre-roasted green bell peppers, sliced
One large onion, chopped
Some dried nettles (optional)
A clove of garlic, minced
Three large eggs, beaten
A large potato, cut into half-inch cubes
Some spinach (wild or otherwise) sliced
Two good pinches of paprika (or more to taste)
Some seasoning
Some olive oil

Method

1. Put the cubes of potato in some salted boiling water until cooked through but still firm
2. Heat some oil in a heavy frying pan and add the onions. Cook till transparent but do not let them become brown.
3. Add the peppers and keep the mix stirring
4. Add the potatoes
5. Add the garlic
6. Add the nettles(or not)
7. Add the spinach
8. Keep stirring
9. Add salt and pepper
10. Add the paprika to the beaten egg mixture
11. Pour the egg mixture over the other ingredients in the pan, and keep stirring
12. Remove from heat when eggs are not runny but not overcooked
13. Serve immediately with crusty bread

Given the country's history, it's understandable that Bulgarian cuisine has been influenced by Turkish and Greek tastes; that though, does not explain the regular appearance of desserts we associate with France and Austria. The latest governmental health-of-the-nation statement confirms that more than ninety percent of Bulgarians over sixty have few or no teeth, and this may well be because of their liking for sugary desserts.

To say Bulgarians have a sweet tooth is like saying that rain is wet, and *crème caramel*, *crêpes* and *baklava* are menu regulars and home favourites. *Banitsa* is a sort-of Bulgarian take on *baklava*, and comes in many guises. It is made by layering whisked eggs and filo pastry with a variety of fillings. On festive occasions, lucky charms may be included. *Banitsa* is eaten hot or cold at any time of day, and may be filled with cheese or spinach or even pumpkin. This is one of the many sweet varieties:

Saraliya Баница
Saraliya Banitsa
(stuffed flaky pastry)

Ingredients

One kg of flour
Two cups of walnut kernels
Four cups of sugar
Six cups of water
A packet of vanilla
Two tablespoons of butter
A pinch of salt

Method

1. Combine the flour and salt and three cups of the water
2. Roll into thin sheets
3. Baste each sheet with butter and top with crushed walnuts
4. Roll the sheets into tubes and arrange in a butter-lined dish
5. Bake for a little over half an hour in a hot oven (375°F)
6. After your banitsas have cooled, pour over the hot syrup made from combining the sugar, three cups of water and the packet of vanilla

PS: *Purists serve this version of banitsa cold. People like me can't wait and also use shop-bought filo pastry.*

Извън пътя
Off the Road

Perhaps, like me, Kom had a heavy night.

It is even hotter than yesterday, though at this height the air is still sharp. The great dome of sky above the valley is unremittingly blue, but the mountain range is wearing a wreath of black cloud. Amplified by the bowl of the valley, a regular rumbling growl of displeasure rolls across the tree tops to where I sit on the balcony trying out a traditional Bulgarian way to start the day.

It is common to any civilisation that hangover cures must taste unpleasant, and I can think of no other reason for drinking a glass of *boza* than for medicinal purposes. Helping take the taste away is a tumbler of very cold and salted yogurt called *Ayran*, which is much nicer than I thought it would be.

Another giant grunt of dyspeptic displeasure echoes around the valley, and great, fat drops of warm rain plop down upon the breakfast table. If I were in Pompeii in 79 AD or steaming past Krakatoa in 1883 I would be concerned, but as far as I know Kom is not and never has been a volcano. Perhaps he knows we will be having our first encounter later today and is sending out warnings that he is not in a receptive mood. I am not too worried, as the only climbing I shall be doing will be by car up the steep mountain roads to his domain.

~

Even at this early hour I find what amounts to a traffic jam in the lane outside. The bundle of clothing I now know to conceal my near neighbour the goat lady is taking her charges for breakfast, and they are impeding the progress of an elderly coffin-cart. The donkey drawing it and the man sitting on it look about the same age in their respective measurements of lifespan. Behind them in the queue is a relatively new Mercedes mini-bus. The next-door dog lies in the middle of the road, lazily observing the drama.

Since arriving, I have realised how free-spirited and independent and therefore cool donkeys are. Bulgarians must think so too, as one was put up for election in the mayoral contest in the nearby town of Varna in 2011. His campaign manager said that unlike the other candidates and the incumbent mayor, Marko had a strong character, did not lie or steal and got things done.

I have already seen that, contrary to popular misconception, donkeys are not at all stupid. It is just that they like to go their own way, and are indifferent to adverse weather, terrain, and above all, the wishes of their masters. This one is clearly doing its own thing and could give The Fonz lessons in laid-backedness. In his *Travels with a Donkey in the Cévennes*, Robert Louise Stevenson admitted losing his temper and repeatedly beating the eternally recalcitrant Modestine. But this owner clearly takes the Elenko managerial approach. He started by shouting, then talking sternly, and now he is wheedling. Eventually, the *magare* twitches its ears, shakes its head, gives a deep sigh and clops on through the gaggle of goats. As he passes, the man looks at me and gives an exasperated what-are-they-like? shrug, and I see that one side of his face is badly disfigured. From below the right eye to the jawline is an angry purple, and it looks as if it could be an aggressive form of skin cancer. He sees my sympathetic and involuntary wince and gives another shrug, then returns to pretending to be in charge of where he and the donkey are going.

When the way is clear, the driver of the Mercedes pulls over to the verge, narrowly missing the dog. It is ignoring me as well as the traffic as it has clearly not made its mind up whether I am to be friend or foe. Even though I slept the sleep of the inebriated last night, I heard it barking regularly in the small hours. Clearly, it needs its sleep in the day so it can be on barking duty after dark.

Before I can try and win favour with a tit-bit from the bag of kitchen waste I am taking to the village bin, there is a cacophonous roar which to my practiced ear can only be caused by a combination of over-revving, crashing gears and a terminally distressed exhaust pipe. I step hurriedly on to the verge as round the bend and on the wrong side of the road hurtles a spectacularly abused white van. Through the deeply scarred and muddy windscreen I see that it appears to be driven by the current president of the Russian Federation.

As I stumble backwards, Ivalin takes both hands off the wheel and waves them maniacally through the aperture where the driver's window would normally be. It is as if he is taking huge delight in driving madly, and I wonder if this is why he also likes risking his life by climbing mountains in casual clothing. As the van clatters by and bits of it bounce off the road I see through the side window that he is ferrying his Roma lady workers to his secret strawberry fields in the foothills outside the village. They turn to look impassively at me, and only one returns my smile and wave. We have not yet met, but I have been invited by Ivalin to join them on a day in the fields.

Peace returns, then there is a heavy creaking as the rusty tennis court-type gate in the fence fronting my neighbour's house opens. A slight, small figure emerges and walks briskly up the slope towards the waiting van.

Sally says that, like most of the women in the village, Madame-next-door is a long-time widow. Her children visit from Sofia at weekends to bring groceries and tend the small family vineyard, but otherwise she receives no visitors and rarely leaves the house. Like the old lady I saw with the walking sticks, my neighbour is wearing a long, loose-fitting top, but her head is bare. Her grey hair is short and immaculately kept and frames a striking face. Because of the lack of surplus flesh and the strength of bone structure, her pale skin seems unlined. I assume she is going to get into the mini-bus, but as she arrives at the top of the slope a hand appears through the driver's window. It is holding a couple of packets of cigarettes, which my neighbour takes. A few words are exchanged, and the driver pulls away as the lady turns back towards the house. I wonder if she heard me staggering home late last night, so I smile and try a much-practiced *Dobro youtro*.

I am quite good at mimicry, but rubbish at remembering more than a handful of useful words and phrases in most foreign languages. The problem with being able to say ' Good morning' in a pretty convincing accent is that the person you are addressing will naturally assume you are familiar with the rest of the words in his or her language. Madame-next-door clearly does, and lets fly with a stream of what could be pleasantries about the weather or invectives for disturbing her sleep by giving her dog cause to bark. After a while she pauses and looks at me expectantly. I inevitably fall back on the alternate idiot grin and frown of sympathy and shake and nod of head which I hope will cover a suitable positive or negative response to whatever she has been saying. Eventually, she sighs, shakes her head as if in sympathy for my obvious mental disability and walks back down the slope. As she does not set the dog on me, I assume she is assuming I am harmless.

~

I have found the large swing-top rubbish bin which serves this part of the village. Although it is hot, there is none of the usual smell you would expect from the domestic waste of at least twenty properties. I lift the lid and see that the bin is acting as more of a compost heap than a refuse collector. The bottom is covered with no more than a layer of broken branches and some withered plant cuttings. Unlike anywhere in Britain, the people of this village obviously waste nothing, including what we would classify as rubbish.

Turning back toward the guest house, I see a figure on the other side of the road; it is standing on tiptoe on the verge while belabouring a tree with a long stick.

As well as having something against this particular tree, its assailant seems unusually dressed even for a Balkan village. The man is no bigger than an adolescent child, and everything he wears seems at least two sizes too big. His heavy boots are unlaced, and I can see he is wearing no socks as his trousers have been hauled up and belted at chest level. Just to be sure, he wears braces as well, and the effect is of a very small fisherman in oversized waders. Like the goat lady, he clearly feels the cold in spite of the heat of the day, and under the braces he is wearing a heavy roll-neck sweater of the sort favoured by Royal Navy submariners in World War II. On the back of his head is what looks like the sort of magnificently over-the-top vertically-peaked cap a Red Army officer of at least Colonel rank would wear.

From under it emerges a shower of black curls, cascading over small, delicately sculpted ears. The man, who looks to be in his thirties, has an equally small and finely shaped nose above a long upper lip. He is clean shaven, though dark stubble shows against his heavily-tanned face. The most remarkable thing about his appearance is his eyes. They are large and deep set and heavily lidded, and the pupils are so dark they appear almost black. He seems to be studying me with a mixture of uncertainty and curiosity, like an animal which is used to humans but still cautious in their presence.

As I smile and nod reassuringly, he lowers the long stick and swings it towards me.

I step back and then see that the end of the stick has been whittled down to fit into the neck of a plastic bottle. The bottom of the bottle has been cut off, and in the remaining half is an orange-coloured fruit which looks like a cross between an apricot and a curiously-coloured plum. I realise that the little man is not trying to fend me off, but is offering to share his breakfast. I reach out, take the plum and bite into it. It is unripe, but I ape pleasure and pat my stomach and smile. He does not respond, but continues to regard me with his unsure look. I lift a hand slowly, then back away. He looks relieved, then turns back to the tree.

I walk back home, throwing the fruit stone at the dog next door as I pass. People say nothing happens in remote villages, but I cannot imagine life ever being boring in Krasiva.

~

A day out with Sally and Richard and their family car.

Unless they come off the production lines already pre-distressed, dented and coated in mud, Ladas must have a hard life from birth. For sure I have never seen even a new one that looks cared for.

There is something unmistakably Eastern European about the workmanlike box-shaped design, and Ladas are seen everywhere on this side of what used to be called the Iron Curtain. Twenty million units were churned out in the last two decades of the Soviet era, and in the West they became a much-mocked symbol of dreary, unimaginative Russian pragmatism.

But they are cheap and easy to run, maintain and repair, and seem to go on forever. I don't think it would be too fanciful to say that, for their rural Bulgarian owners, they are the donkey of modern times. They are made to be worked hard, and the advantage over a donkey is that they generally do what they are told. Even after death they continue to serve their masters as garden sheds or hen houses. I suppose it is because they are such reliable and faithful servants that they engender affection in their owners more than many other makes.

Richard and Sally seem as fond of their battered Niva 1996 4 x 4 as Elenko is of Chiro the donkey. I know it has taken them thousands of miles safely around the Balkans and often across terrain which would have daunted a Sherman tank. It has also literally survived fire and flood. The fire was when a local mechanic thought it a good idea to strap some new wiring against the exhaust pipe, and the flood was when Richard tried to ford a previously unexplored river which turned out to be deeper than the roof of the car.

I can understand their affection and have had my share of old and previously neglected cars. My first was a 1939 Ford I bought for a fiver, no questions asked. In those pre-MOT days it was enough that a car had a wheel in each corner to be roadworthy, and until one fell off while I was driving, Freddie was a loyal servant and friend.

For sure, the Moore's Lada is one of the most distressed but still mobile cars I have seen in modern times, and that is saying something. It is or was red, and sales returns show this was the most popular colour in Bulgaria. Some claim this was because bloodstains would not be so noticeable. This car was imported from

England so the steering wheel is on the right hand side, and that is not an unusual situation here. It is one of the vagaries of market supply and demand that it can be cheaper to buy a car in England, drive it 1600 miles through seven countries and register it in Bulgaria. Also curiously, drivers seem to have no objection to having their steering wheel on the wrong side. In fact it is said that some prefer it as most serious accidents or deaths in head-on crashes are suffered by the drivers. When you are in control of the car from the nearside seat, it's the passenger who has the problem.

~

If she is embarrassed by the man inspecting her teats at very close quarters, the cow does not show it. She is placidly chewing the cud and ignoring the figure lying beneath her. His feet are below her front legs, and his head beneath her great swollen udders. At first I think it might be a crafty Bulgarian wheeze for sheltering from the sun on a hot day, then see that his nose is no more than an inch from one of the cow's teats.

Hearing our approach, the man quickly rolls over and out from under and sits up as we drive by. He gives us an almost sheepish look, then turns to place one hand on the cow's belly while tapping the back of it with two fingers like a doctor checking a patient for fluid in the lungs. We drive on, and Sally charitably suggests he was lying under his cow to check her udders and teats for mastitis. Richard sniffs and says he may not even be the owner, and he was sure the man wiped his mouth guiltily as he sat up. Perhaps, he says, he was having a free drink straight from source.

~

In his other life, Richard Moore was an accountant.

Retirement has given him the opportunity to leave behind all the conformity necessary to his former profession, and he has taken full advantage of it. Or perhaps he was always a free spirit, trapped in a suit.

For whatever reason, he is clearly a one-off; coming to Bulgaria has amplified his innate eccentricity, and he seems to be making up for all the straight years. He appears to dress in whatever clothes are nearest to hand in the morning, and has the general appearance of a man you would give a pound to if your eyes met in a shopping precinct.

In reality he is a man of huge intelligence and depth, enhanced by a very dry sense of humour. He probably knows more about Bulgaria's complex past than most of the country's history teachers, and is interested in everything. He is also a complete all-rounder when it comes to building crafts, and can wipe a joint quicker than I can make a cup of tea.

His eccentricity comes to the fore when behind the wheel, and there is something Jeckyll and Hyde-ish about his approach to driving. On the village roads he is considerate and fast but never furious. Off-road, he cannot pass a piece of terrain which would deter a Panzer tank.

Minutes ago, we were avoiding potholes and lizards on the road to Krasiva; now we are bucketing across the wild foothills of the Balkans, and civilisation lies far behind. This will be, Richard explains as we come as close to a vehicle's tipping point as I have ever been, his third attempt to find an alleged short-cut to the nearest town.

Berkovitsa is a little more than six miles from Krasiva by what they call a road in Bulgaria. Richard believes the local legend that an old track through the foothills halves the distance. It is said that many villagers used to walk across the river and alongside the forest to town on market day. If they survived drowning, attacks by brigands, wolves or bears, they could make the journey in an hour.

Richard has not met anyone - including Ivalin - who has made the journey by foot or donkey cart in recent years, and certainly not by car. It is said that several outsiders have taken up the challenge over the years, but they and their vehicles have never been seen again. Either they made it through and did not bother to return to reveal the secret of the southerly passage, or they languish still somewhere in the deep, dark depths of the forest, skeletal hands still gripping the cobwebbed steering wheels.

~

We have crossed two rivers and a stream, or it may be that we have crossed the same water course three times. There seem to be few distinct features to set a course by, as one tree looks much like another and there are thousands to choose from.

We left a deeply rutted tractor track half an hour ago, and are now bumping over virgin hillside. It is quite possible that man has never set foot here, and highly unlikely that any vehicle has travelled this way unless it be one of the cars that never returned. Richard says we are not lost as we can only be a few miles from the village, but I think that is a technicality. The sun is directly overhead, so not much help in determining which way we are heading. I seem to remember that moss grows only on one side of trees and indicates a compass point, but not which side or at which compass point. Richard says he bought a GPS system at a boot sale recently, but could not understand the Bulgarian instructions so leaves it at home. Sally has been going through the debris on the floor of the Lada and has found a half-filled bottle of water and two cough sweets which she says she will ration to help extend our survival time.

Then, suddenly, we see signs of civilisation. It is not a

Roman ruin, an abandoned homestead, or even a rusting car. It is a giant, three-legged water tank, lying on its side like a mortally-wounded Martian tripod in *The War of the Worlds*.

Beyond it is a track, and beyond that the sunlight twinkles on the roofs of moving cars. Richard is clearly unhappy not to have found the secret passage to town, and even to have to leave the switchback terrain. I cannot remember when I was so pleased to see a busy road, savagely potholed or not.

~

We are back on route to Kom, but there has been a temporary delay.

We entered the dual carriageway further away from the town of Berkovitsa than if we had stuck to the usual route, and now we sit at a flimsy barrier as a train lumbers by. The single track runs alongside the road, and carries a series of passenger carriages that are pulled to and from the town of Montana several times a day. Where the track crosses the looping road there are minimal cautionary notices. To be fair they are hardly necessary, as the train appears to travel no faster than a man with a bad leg could walk.

Curiously, there is a complete absence of frustrated parping or arm-waving from the cars lined up at the barrier. It is almost as if the drivers are enjoying the break from trying to maim or kill each other when the road is clear. Some get out of their vehicles and exchange pleasantries and cigarettes, and one man is showing off photos of his daughter's recent wedding. It puts me in mind of the Christmas Day truces in the trenches of World War I, and I half expect someone to produce a football and start a kick-about.

This is another intriguing insight into the Bulgarian psyche. They would die rather than get stuck behind a slow vehicle on the mountain pass for a few minutes, but are not unhappy to be held up for much longer when the road is blocked. Perhaps it is that they have learned over a long history of occupation, oppression, communism and general hard times that there is no point in getting angry or upset in the face of the inevitable.

~

It has been an extended stop at the barrier, as the train has picked up a passenger. An elderly lady was standing by a pile of sleepers lying alongside the track near the barrier, and the driver had attempted to pull up so the makeshift platform was directly in line with one of the carriage doors. His first attempt had overshot the mark, so he put the train in reverse, then jumped down from the cab and walked back to help her through the door. With a hearty push he got her on board, and she handed him a small brown paper package through the window.

He touched his forehead, tucked the package away in the top pocket of his bib and brace overalls, then strode back to the cab. There were a couple of toots from drivers as he pulled away, and it was not clear if they were of irritation at the extra delay, or appreciation of his assistance to the elderly passenger.

The train gone with a blast from its hooter, the barriers creaked up and we were on our way. I have seen these curious little incidents happen all over Europe in rural areas, and it is frustrating that I can never know the story behind them.

Perhaps the old lady was the driver's mother and was giving him his sandwiches before taking a ride into town to do some shopping. Or it could be that she was a drug dealer in disguise, handing over the latest batch of crack cocaine to be distributed in Berkovitsa. Never knowing the story behind these small moments of interaction can be a disappointment, but also strangely engaging.

~

We are passing through the outskirts of Berkovitsa, and Sally says it is the area where what are officially known as 'domesticated' Roma live. It is from here that Ivalin recruits labour for his strawberry and raspberry harvesting.

In spite of or perhaps because of who occupies most of the neighbourhood, signs at the start of each street leading off the main road show a horse and cart with a red line through them. The residents don't seem to take much notice, as many houses have a donkey and cart parked outside.

The traffic slows as we negotiate a string of Roma families travelling in single file. The lead cart is drawn by a pony which trots with an unnatural high-stepping gait. I wonder if there is status to having a horse rather than a donkey pull your cart, and if the driver is the leader of a local tribe. He is a big, muscular chap, with a proud, hawk-like profile. The woman beside him on the cart seems particularly laden with bracelets, necklaces and all sorts of bangles and beads. As we overtake, I see there is a bed sheet knotted around the pony's neck. It passes beneath its tail and the corners are attached to each side of the front of the cart. It looks like a giant nappy, and Sally says that some policemen stop Roma carts and make the owners clean up any droppings. Perhaps the sheet is there to avoid that indignity, or perhaps the owner wants to save any manure for his vegetable garden. Or, as Sally suggests, to throw at unsympathetic policemen.

~

We have reached the mountain heights and another road block.

An apparently limitless phalanx of tall trees hems us in

on both sides, and our passage is blocked by a flatbed Soviet-era lorry. It is clearly aged but massively built and looks untroubled by the giant stack of logs it bears.

Beside the lorry, three scruffily-dressed men are lined up facing a short, portly figure in a green uniform. They do not have their hands in the air or on their heads, but are clearly being rigorously questioned. Beyond the group stands a man in a blue uniform and his hand rests on the butt of his holstered hand gun. Behind him, two seriously off-road vehicles are drawn up nose-to-nose to hinder any traffic from getting through without official sanction. One is a Nissan with huge tyres which would not have looked out of place on a tractor. The bodywork is almost as scarred as our Lada, is covered with mud and bristling with fixed and mobile lamps, winches and other manly pieces of off-road kit. I can almost hear Richard salivating. Taking in the scene, it looks as if the man in blue is acting as a minder for the man in green, and Sally explains that one is from the Forestry Patrol, and the other a member of the Border Patrol.

In 2012 there was an outcry and series of huge demonstrations in Sofia when an amendment to Bulgaria's Forest Act proposed allowing private individuals to buy and develop huge swathes of state-owned forest for ski-slopes or golf courses. The new owners would be allowed to build in previously protected areas and could even receive grants for denuding the land. The amendments were dropped after a tsunami of protest, and the event showed the strength of public opinion and how ordinary Bulgarians value the forests that cover a third of their land.

Some feel so strongly about the forests being the property of the people that they help themselves generously to winter fuel. As Richard says, nobody is too worried about an individual loading the back of his car with fallen branches, but organised tree-theft on a massive scale is big business.

It is clear that the forestry patrol man suspects that the driver of the lorry has no permit to cut down and take away such a large quantity of wood, and the man in blue is there to back him up.

The armed guard is clearly bored, and after a while hitches up his pants and goes to talk to his colleague. They both turn and look our way, then the border guard walks towards where we sit. He is tall and broad with a massive moustache which matches his obvious sense of self-importance. I assume that he is going to wave us through, but instead he looks through the windscreen at us and then points brusquely at the side of the road.

We pull over and the man walks slowly around the battered Lada, then signals for Richard to wind down his window. This is not easy as there is no knob on the winder, but Richard takes a bent six-inch nail from the glove box, slips it through the hole where the knob should fit and the window creaks down. The slowness of his response seems to irritate the officer, who lets off a machine-gun volley of words to which Richard replies with the single word 'angleeskee'. This seems to irritate the man even more. After an exasperated shake of his head, he puts his palms together then opens them in a mime demanding to see some identity.

While we fiddle with pockets and wallets, Sally says that she thinks the man thinks we may be illegal immigrants. She is wearing a very ethnic, flowing dress, and Richard and I are sporting beards and, to be frank, could easily be taken for particularly poorly dressed would-be refugees.

The severely abused Lada does not lend us an air of respectability. As I smile disarmingly at the policeman and go through my pockets for my passport, I remember that Serbia is not a member of the European Union, and lies only a couple of miles away cross-country.

A growing number of refugees and illegal immigrants see Bulgaria as an entry point to the EU, and increasingly strong action has been taken to deter them.

Such is the strength of feeling among people living near the borders that vigilante groups have been formed to detain migrants and alert the authorities. One group calls itself the Organisation for the Protection of Bulgarian Citizens, and some of its members sport paramilitary outfits. In spite of this impingement on what should be official territory, the groups' activities have been recognised and even rewarded by the border police. Ironically, it is only a couple of decades since Bulgaria tore down the fences that the communist regime put up to keep people in. Recently, a hundred-mile length of fencing was erected on the border with Turkey to keep refugees or would-be economic migrants out.

The border guard is looking increasingly irate, and has taken to chewing the ends of his massive moustache as well as idling with the strap keeping his gun in its holster. He takes and inspects Richard and Sally's residency cards, screws up his face as if disappointed, then hands them back. Then he leans down and looks into the back of the car and at me, sticking one stubby-fingered hand through the window. I think quickly as I riffle through my wallet and discard the idea of presenting him with a credit card in case he thinks I am trying to bribe him. My international driving licence and passport are in a drawer at the guest house, and I think I may be in trouble. Then I come across a laminated card with lots of official-looking letters and numbers and my photograph on it. I take it from its holder and hand it to the policeman as if it were a very special document. He looks at it and then me, nods grudgingly and gives it back. Finally, he stands away, waves us through, and watches as we squeeze past the lorry and through the gap between the two 4x4s.

I sit back and wipe my brow and consider how fortunate it was that, however unnecessarily, I brought my senior citizen's free bus pass with me to the hinterlands of Bulgaria.

~

The best-known and most popular Bulgarian ski resort is in the south-west.

Bansko has what is generally agreed to be the finest ski centre, the longest ski season and the best snow record. There are 44 snow cannons to make sure the surfaces are always to the pitch of perfection, and skiers can get to the top of the runs with fast chair and drag lifts and even a sophisticated gondola-type cable car.

Sadly, the local slope hardly matches that level of excellence, though it was the great white hope for the Montana region. The idea was to create a rival to Bansko on the slopes of the Stara Planina above the former spa town of Berkovitsa. Huge investment was going to rejuvenate the town and area and bring prosperity along with flocks of snowboarders and ski-ists in search of a budget holiday.

For some reason, the investment plan faltered and the dreams of a world-class ski centre have yet to materialise. It does not help that there is no real snow at this time of year, but at the moment the would-be rival to Bansko looks more like an abandoned mining settlement than a luxury ski destination.

A scruffy caravan sits beneath what looks like an elderly beam engine and which I assume drives the drag lift. There were to be cable cars taking customers up to the top of the runs, but like the tunnel from Sofia and the proposed helicopter pad for mega-wealthy patrons, they have yet to materialise.

Across the clearing is a huddle of chalets, some of which are literally roofless and otherwise derelict. I fear even the better-maintained ones would have drawn complaints from visitors to Butlins in the unfussy mid-1950's.

The average review of Bansko on a popular winter sports enthusiasts' website is three out of five stars.

Berkovitsa does not even rate a mention. Like any good idea which has faltered and failed for lack of investment or intent, it is sad to see what is on offer here and think about what might have been.

~

Close to the slopes is an hotel that Richard thinks may have been a former communist holiday camp. It certainly has the familiar no-nonsense design of that era, though is not dissimilar to the sort of cube-like budget hotels which sprout nowadays alongside motorways in the UK. Unlike the car park of the average Premier Inn, this one is occupied by two very modern and expensive-looking snow ploughs, and a small mountain of felled tree trunks.

Two men are working on the pile, one with a chain saw and the other a felling axe.

The man with the chain saw becomes aware of us, and walks over with the engine still idling and the chain looping slowly round. Close behind him is the man with the axe. I consider the possibility that they have made the same mistake as the Border Patrol officer, and because of the Lada and our appearance have mistaken us for would-be illegal migrants. It may even be that they are members of the local branch of the Organisation for the Protection of Bulgarian Citizens. The man with the chain saw looks quite friendly, but his companion has something of the manic air and wild eyes of Jack Nicholson before he smashed through the door in the winter sports hotel in *The Shining*.

They arrive, and Richard says a few words in Bulgarian, accompanied by the international mime for eating and drinking. I am pleased to see that the smaller man turns his chain saw off before replying. The younger man still grips the long shaft of his chopper tightly, but the mad gleam in his eyes has faded.

After a further exchange, Richard explains that the hotel

is shut, but the man with the chain saw says his wife is making the midday meal and we are welcome if we're prepared to have what they are having.

We exchange looks and I give the thumbs up. Some of the best meals I have had in foreign countries are when I have eaten what the staff is having. We follow the chain saw man into the vestibule, while the Jack Nicholson lookalike returns to his work.

At the reception desk, our host - who may be the owner, manager or off-season caretaker - points toward a pair of tall, glass panelled doors. As I push one open, I see a small sticker at eye level. It bears no words, but the two illustrations make its meaning clear. Both of the silhouettes have red lines through them; one is the outline of a dog while the other is of a hand gun. It is clear that the management prefers customers to leave their hunting hounds outside, and like a respectable saloon in the Wild West, the rule is that all shooting irons must be checked in before entry.

~

We find ourselves in a high-ceilinged rectangular dining hall that is reminiscent of a college refectory or factory canteen of the 1970s. One of the longer walls is windowed from floor to ceiling and looks out on to a yard where another pristine snow plough sits. Beyond lies the ski slope, which must be a seductive sight for keen skiers at breakfast in the season. The other wall has a return-swing door which leads to the kitchen, and alongside is a serving counter and bar. High on a shelf, a stuffed owl eyes us suspiciously. Lining the hall are ranks of long, plywood-topped tables, each with a large bunch of plastic flowers. Full, there would be room for more than a hundred diners.

Sally's artistic eye is caught immediately by a superbly-tooled Turkish wooden ceiling area which looks completely out of place in the utilitarian surroundings. I am drawn to another unusual feature, which is a very big and ornate stove. It echoes the hall in its rectangular shape, gleams from much polishing and bristles with dials and levers. There are doors on the front, but the most curious attachment is the huge, four-bladed propeller attached to the back. At first I wonder if it is to make the stove self-propelling, as it would certainly be too heavy to move without a block and tackle. Then I realise it is an ingenious device for getting maximum benefit from the warmth created by the stove. The fan is on gimbals, so can be moved easily to direct the hot air to any corner of the hall. The temperature outside is around 25 degrees Centigrade so I will not be able to see this magnificent creation working. I make a mental note to return in the season, and join Sally and Richard at a window with a view of the chestnut forest.

~

We have dined very well, and are sitting in the empty hall, perhaps surrounded by the ghosts of the thousands of Bulgarian workers who could have taken a compulsory holiday here. If it was a worker's vacation centre I would like to be able to ask them if they enjoyed the break, or resented it as it was not of their choice of time or place. Things were different even in those comparatively recent times, and I suspect that any holiday would have been gratefully accepted. Montana was a stronghold of the communist movement, and it would not have been a good idea to show dissent.

The hotel* is a fascinating reminder of Bulgaria's past, and in a striking location. But given the state of the ski slope I wonder how well it does in the season now that people have to pay to stay here. Sally says it is up for sale, and going very cheap. Elsewhere in Europe, a hotel alongside a ski slope would be snapped up for millions.

This one is on sale at the price of a modest flat above a fried fish and chip shop in a not-so-desirable borough of London.

I thank our host in sign language and pay the bill. Coincidentally, lunch and drinks for four of us comes to about the same as a single portion of fish and chips from a shop in a not-so-desirable borough of London

I discovered later that what I thought was an hotel is actually a hostel. There are 37,000 kilometres of marked hiking trails in and across the national parks and reserves of Bulgaria, and the Kom-Ermine trail follows the ridge of the Balkans eastwards for 450 miles to where it ends at Cape Ermine on the Black Sea. It typically takes 20-25 days to complete and features 30 mountain huts like the one we dined in at the base of Kom.

They vary in size from a basic shelter to something as comparatively luxurious as the Kom Hut, and they get some very mixed reviews. I found one description of facilities at a hut which proudly announced that the bathrooms had baths and floors. There are often reports of drunken behaviour and lack of attention to hygiene standards by both management and visitors. Intriguingly there are also tales of some very odd managers or owners presiding over the most isolated premises. Perhaps that is why I got a frisson of uneasiness with the appearance of the man with the axe when we arrived at the Kom Hut.

Apart from shelter and sustenance, the most attractive aspect of the Hut system is the price. A night's stay can be less than ten pounds, and lunch as little as five leva (£2). That's why I queried our bill for dining at the Kom Hut. Not because it seemed expensive, but because it seemed too cheap.

Unsurprisingly, our tasty meal at the hotel/hostel was accompanied by lashings of white bread. But this was a special, home-made cheesy variety that our hosts were buttering with a red, very spicy relish before dipping it in their soup.

The relish/pickle is called *lyutinitsa*, and has several preferred spellings. It can be found in grocery shops throughout Bulgaria, but many families prefer to make their own. Like many Bulgarian favourites, lyutinitsa demonstrates the people's liking for strong flavours - and lots of salt. The recipe for what I suppose we would call souped-up tomato chutney varies from region to region, and some call for aubergines to be added. 'Lyut' means 'hot' or 'spicy', so be warned. This is a basic recipe for a year's worth and will be more than quite hot for some tastes, so make the necessary amendments if you prefer less bulk and a milder flavour:

лютеница
Lyutinitsa
(spicy tomato relish)

Ingredients

A kg of red sweet pepper
A kg of tomatoes
Two cups of olive oil
Two cups of sugar
20 hot chillies, ground
A third of a cup of salt

Method

1. Roast the red peppers, seed and peel and grind coarsely

2. Roughly slice the tomatoes and fry with the peppers for ten minutes
3. Add the sugar and the salt and some water and let the mixture thicken
4. During the thickening process add the ground chillies.
5. Bottle and eat cold.

тутманик
Tutmanik
(cheesy bread)

The bread, like the rest of our meal, was home-made, and this cheesy version really hit the spot when liberally spread with the tomato and pepper relish and dunked in the soup. Also known as *mesenitza*, the recipe varies, but the basic components remain bread and feta-type cheese*:

Ingredients

One cup of plain yogurt
Two eggs
300g of crumbled feta-style cheese (*sirene*)
A quarter of a cup of olive oil
Half a teaspoon of salt
A tablespoon of sugar
Two cups of flour
Half a teaspoon of baking soda
One teaspoon of baking powder
A half teaspoon of paprika
A teaspoon of caraway seeds

Method

1. Mix together in a bowl the yogurt, eggs, feta, oil, salt and sugar
2. Sift together the flour, baking powder and baking soda
3. Slowly add the yogurt and mix well
4. Pour into a well-greased 9 inch x 9 inch baking dish
5. Lightly sprinkle with paprika and caraway seeds

6. Bake in a pre-heated oven at 400°F for twenty minutes or until a toothpick comes out clean

this cheesy bread is not to be confused with banitza (see earlier recipe), which can be made with feta-style cheese trapped in layers of filo pastry.

Боб Чорба
Bob Chorba
(bean soup)

I suppose Bulgarian bean soup will not be everyone's idea of *hauté cuisine,* but then I bet they have not tried it. Bob Chorba is not a rock god or football star, but probably the most common and popular dish in the nation's cuisine. The 'monastery version' is meatless, but some people like to add a little smoked ham. That is how we had it at the Kom Hut.

This star of the Bulgarian soup pantheon comes in a variety of sizes and names and is part of a huge family. The navy or pea bean was domesticated in America, and is one the smallest of the white beans. The Italians like their cannellini beans, which are larger than the navy variety and related to the good old kidney bean. The great northern or 'large white' has a similar flavour to lima beans. The Greeks have a word for their big uncle to the runner bean, which is *gigantes*. This recipe makes for more than a gallon, so invite plenty of friends to share the feast:

Ingredients

300g of dried great northern (or similar) beans, soaked for six hours, then rinsed and cooked for the best part of an hour
Two tablespoons of olive oil
A cup of chopped onion
A cup of chopped carrot
A cup of chopped celery
Two cloves of garlic, finely chopped
Half a teaspoon of crushed red pepper flakes
Two tablespoons of sweet paprika

Some salt
Some pepper
Five cups of water
Five cups of chicken broth
A large smoked ham hock
Half a cup of fresh mint
Half a cup of chopped flat leaf parsley

Method

1. After cooking the beans, heat the oil in a large soup pot and add the onion, celery, carrot and garlic. Cook until the onion is soft
2. Add the red pepper, salt, paprika and black pepper and sauté for a few minutes
3. Add the water, chicken broth and ham hock, bring to the boil and simmer for around an hour, partially covered
4. Remove the ham hock and let cool
5. Turn off the heat and add the beans, mint and parsley to the soup
6. Use a hand blender to break up the beans a bit, or take some out and mash them before returning to the pot
7. Remove the meat from the hock, dice it finely and add to the pot
8. Simmer your *bob chorba*, and season to taste with pepper and salt and paprika

Boza is the traditional breakfast drink I tried on my first morning in Krasiva, and is a popular way to start the day in virtually all the south-eastern European countries. It is said to have originated in the time of the Ottoman Empire, and apart from curing hangovers, regular consumption is claimed to boost the immune system and even increase the size of a woman's breasts. This is because the melange is rich in vitamins A, B and E and can raise the natural level of the hormone prolactin, which promotes maternal milk production. There are various favourite recipes, and this is a basic and simple one:

Боза
(boza)

Ingredients

250g corn flour
4 litres of warm water
10g yeast
250g sugar

Method

1. Put the corn flour in a large pot with three litres of the water and leave overnight
2. Next morning, put on a low heat and cook for two hours, stirring occasionally
3. Take from heat and allow to stand for two hours
4. Stir yeast into the other litre of water and then add to the flour mixture and allow to ferment till the next day
5. Strain the liquid and add the sugar, then put in bottles and keep in the fridge

Втори дом
Home from Home

People who live near the sea often laud its ever-changing appearance and say how impossible it would be for them to live inland.

Until I came to Krasiva I would have agreed, but being here has altered my view in more ways than one. Most of the scenery here may not move, but it changes continually and can be quite as dramatic as any Turner seascape.

I am taking my morning walk along the high road, and the air is so clear and the light so intense that it enhances textures and shades and brings everything into sharp focus. I am almost intoxicated by the way the translucence draws me into the landscape, and feel I could almost reach out and touch the forest a mile away.

As I think about the advantages of having the powers of the man with the elastic limbs in The Fantastic Four, I see a figure moving among the rows of brightly coloured beehive boxes which line the slopes of this part of the valley. He is not wearing special protective clothing or even gloves, just a wide-brimmed straw hat, a shirt with the sleeves rolled up, and a pair of trousers held up by a length of baling twine. After opening a bright yellow box and peering inside, he nods as if satisfied. Even at this distance I can see he is puffing on a fat home-made cigarette, though whether to produce smoke to keep the bees quiet or just for his personal pleasure I do not know.

He senses and sees me watching and waves amicably, then walks over to what looks like a prop from the film of *Far from the Madding Crowd*. It is a mobile shepherd's hut and with its curved roof and square windows it puts me in mind of a small, old fashioned-railway carriage. It sits on large, spoked metal wheels and is painted the same bright green as several of the beehive boxes.

The elderly man takes off his hat and waves goodbye as he sees I am still watching, then climbs the steps and disappears inside. He is obviously using the hut as a garden shed, and I wonder if he would believe me if I told him the going rate for a twee reproduction of the hut in Britain. A current must-have for the gardens of the sort of people who go glamping rather than camping, there are even towable versions so the owners can show other road users how much more money they have than sense.

Continuing along the high road towards the outskirts of the village, I see activity in one of the vineyards lining the upper slopes. A donkey is plodding uphill between two of the rows of precisely spaced and rigidly erect grapevine posts, and it appears to be towing a man holding onto a giant pair of motorcycle handles. As I get closer, I see the handles are attached to a metal ploughshare, which itself is linked by reins and chains to the donkey's harness. Behind the middle-aged man walks a woman who is picking up the weeds excavated by the plough. Now and then they stop and rest from their labours, with the woman standing up straight and stretching her back, and the man taking off his hat and wiping his brow. The donkey does not seem to appreciate the break, and stands waiting to get started again. Or not, if it decides against. It is a scene which can't have changed significantly for centuries, except that there is a small, modern saloon car on the road at the bottom of the slope. Behind it is an old-fashioned open trailer for the donkey's ride home. To me and unlike the fad for fake shepherd's huts, the contrast represents a perfect outcome of mixing the benefits of old and modern ways.

My reverie is disturbed by the sound of a straining engine, and round the corner appears a large man in a bright orange ball cap and a pair of bib-and-brace overalls. He is sitting astride a noisy machine which is pulling a large wooden trailer piled high with hay. As it draws nearer I realise it is a Rotavator which has been adapted to act as a mini-tractor and also a general runabout. I have seen a couple of these curious hybrids in fields alongside the main road and even on the road itself, once taking a whole family in their Sunday best to Berkovitsa. They are obviously cheaper to run than a car, and maybe even a donkey or pony. But I don't think they will ever replace the more traditional method of transport in the countryside, and the figures actually show a growth in the donkey population. In 1990 there were reckoned to be around a hundred thousand nationwide, but the latest estimate is double that. If the trend continues and Bulgarians keep leaving, there could one day be more donkeys than humans here. Depending on your view, this could be a good or bad thing.

I step back on to the verge and the man and his machine chug by. As our eyes meet, he sweeps his *I Love New York* ball cap off his head in a theatrical manner and roars a greeting. I respond with a bow and reach for my camera.

As the noise dies and utter stillness returns, I realise my tally for acknowledgement from strangers in Krasiva and Berkovitsa stands at a hundred percent, and that is without any encouragement from me. When walking along the beach near our home in southern England, I often run a book on how many strangers will respond to my cheery greeting, and if they do, what form it will take. On average, four out of every ten people will refuse to return my greeting. Some will stare fixedly ahead, some will glare at me as if outraged I have dared to address them, while others will avert their eyes and assume a nervous expression as if they fear being accosted. I think this is a sad observation on our modern attitudes, but my wife thinks it is me, and that my victims fear I am an escaped lunatic.

I round the bend and pause to admire the house with the best view in the village.

The whitewashed cottage has a red tiled roof, post-and-rail fencing and a five-barred gate and looks markedly out of place in a Balkan village. It sits on the rim of the valley, by a track which leads past the modern farm building where Ivalin processes his fruit crops. At the end of the track is an abandoned farm, and beyond that the great bowl of the valley and the river and forest. The farm is in a very poor state and has been on sale for years at an almost giveaway price. I know that Richard and Sally considered buying it as a potential arts and crafts centre, but changed their minds after counting the cost of a full restoration even in rural Bulgaria.

The neat little cottage used to be an outbuilding of the derelict farm, but now looks as if it has been uprooted from a rural setting in England and replanted here.

It belongs to an Englishman who bought it as a ruin eight years ago and restored it virtually single-handedly in an image to his liking. He is no longer young, but soon he is to quit his sheltered accommodation in Bristol to spend the rest of his life here. By so doing, he will add to the number of surprisingly few Britons who have decided to live in this fascinating country.

Bulgaria is about the same distance by road or air from Britain as southern Spain; the weather and climate are similar, the landscape at least as attractive and the people probably more friendly, and the cost of living much, much cheaper here. Yet at least half a million Britons choose to live permanently in or own a holiday home in Spain. 300,000 live in France and 45,000 in Greece, which is a neighbour to Bulgaria. It is thought the total of expatriate Britons in this country could be as low as eighteen thousand. If this is true, there are ten times as many Bulgarians living in the UK as there are Britons living in Bulgaria. Like the donkey population situation, this is either a fair exchange or a bad deal depending on your view. On the positive side, it means there are at least forty donkeys for every Briton who has moved here.

Отивате на града
Going to Town

I know that Berkovitsa has the oldest clock tower in the country. I would have a small bet that there are more men with no necks living here than anywhere else in Bulgaria.

The town sits in the valley of the river for which it was named (or vice-versa) at a height of 405 metres on the northern slope of the Starina Planina range. The mighty Kom peak almost literally overshadows the town.

At last count there were about 14,000 people living in the environs of Berkovitsa, and a mere four thousand in the full five hundred square kilometre extent of the municipality. It is also quite possible that the number of Berkovitsans will have diminished in common with the falling national population. I can find no statistics for recent years, so perhaps the authorities do not want to hear or re-broadcast any bad news.

I have been given the official tourist guide to the history and delights of Берковица, but as it is in Bulgarian and Cyrillic to boot it is not very helpful to foreigners.

From my research I know that the town goes back a long way, originally as a Roman settlement complete with fortress and baths. The Byzantines erected one of the first Christian churches here in the 5th century, and the town thrived under Turkish rule as an important trading post because of its location on the shortest route from the Danube river to the Aegean sea. By then it was already famed for its woodworking crafts and produced what was said to be the best pottery in the land.

Nowadays Berkovitsa is billed as a ski resort, though it is unlike any I have ever visited. But then and as I found out yesterday, so is the ski centre on the slopes above the town. To be fair, it is out of season; perhaps when the snow comes the streets will be athrong with people in silly bobble hats and designer dark glasses, spending fortunes in the shops. Somehow and looking at what is on offer in the shops, I doubt it.

Long before someone had the idea of making the town a magnet for winter sports enthusiasts, Berkovitsa was best known as a spa. Its pure mountain air was a selling point from the mid -19th century, and the town became a training camp for famous Bulgarian wrestlers. There is probably no connection, but this sporting legacy may account for the number of men with very big bodies and no necks.

It is a hot day, and like most muscular males they clearly like to show off what they've got, so are wearing very skimpy vests and short shorts. All have the same strange, wide-legged lumbering gait, presumably to avoid major chafing caused by rubbing the insides of their huge thighs together. In contrast, their top halves are held completely still, with massive arms hanging down and away from the bodies like gunfighters preparing for a quick draw. I have counted a handful of these ambling titans in the half hour since we arrived, and another common factor is that all appear to have remarkably small heads. This may be because of the comparative size of their shoulders or their common lack of hair. Perhaps shaven heads are in fashion, or over-consumption of steroids has made them prematurely bald. Reassuringly, none of these monstrous young men seem threatening, and most smile amiably at those they pass. They are it appears, Big Friendly Giants.

There are also signs that the tradition of body-building goes back at least a generation, as many of the older men are carrying a lot of former muscle which has slipped down to be arrested by their low-slung belts.

Earlier I asked Sally if Berkovitsa is a fairly typical Bulgarian town. After thinking about it she said yes and no, and I already think I know what she means.

Most town centres I have visited in Europe share some similarities. They will have a number of carefully preserved reminders of the past in the shape of a church or cathedral, a famous seat of learning or a river which was once a trade route. In most, there will be a tourist-trap street, often cobbled and with quaintly ancient shops selling sometimes breathtakingly expensive goods and souvenirs.

This town does not fit in with any other I have seen, and that is probably because it is the first small eastern European town I have visited. If Berkovitsa is a typical example, someone must have made an absolute killing selling cement and sand in the Soviet Years.

We are standing in Ploschad Slaveikov, a large, paved square with the 18th century clock tower standing out in dramatic contrast to the concrete, cubiform conformity of its surroundings. The square is hemmed in with what look like post-war buildings, most used as propaganda hoardings. As Montana province was a communist hot-spot, this town would have been expected to show willing. A good example is a giant mural on the side of a block of flats overlooking the square. It shows a smug Lenin looking down with paternal affection on a procession of joyous overall-clad workers, most wearing tribute moustaches to his accomplice Stalin.

Reflecting a pre-communist era, the square is dotted

with plinths on which stand spookily lifelike statues of stern men in frock coats and luxuriant facial hair. But what could be an otherwise oppressive ambience is assuaged by fountains, bustling crowds and an impressive floral display. At least four council workers are sharing one hosepipe to water the plants, so the old communist way of ensuring full employment must be dying hard here.

~

Because of the sparse population and lack of shops in the outlying villages, towns like Berkovitsa are very important social gathering centres. Tomorrow is market day, and many hundreds of people will travel in to buy and meet up with friends. By the look of the square, lots have come a day early for a rehearsal.

There are at least four bars and three kiosks around the square, and all are as busy outside as they are empty inside. In France, the customers would be scrutinising passers-by to check out what they were wearing, how much it would have cost and if the wearers were with their spouses or someone else's. Here, hundreds of people are talking, drinking coffee, eating pastries and smoking animatedly, often all at the same time. More middle-aged or older people sit on the concrete benches lining the square or stand talking in groups.

Traffic is barred from the square, and I have become aware of an unaccustomed sound. It took a moment or two for me to realise it is the buzz of conversation. No tinny music from loudspeakers or *basso profundo* thumps from car stereo systems. There is not a pair of earphones in sight, and people are talking for talking's sake.

I came here with a preconception that Slavic people would not be free with words and that they would have a dour look because the economy and standard of living gave them something to look dour about. But this is very much not so. In any home counties market town in Britain, women in designer clothes and wearing grim and suspiciously taut faces and dark glasses would be pulling up in their Range Rovers or striding quickly by with their designer handbags as if late for a vital appointment or behind schedule on their shopping mission. Here, people are just enjoying the sun and conversation over a cold beer or coffee. Perhaps they are making the most of the weather and exposure to other people, or are all on anti-depressants. Or it could be that they have not learned how badly off they are in comparison with nearly every other Euro country. Whatever the reason, it is a delight to be amongst so many real people and I think I am going to like this small and unassuming town.

~

It is a shopkeeping tradition to have samples of stock on show in the window. This is true for most of the shops we have passed, but not this one. The windows are covered in posters showing gleaming washing machines and vacuum cleaners and other domestic goods. As Sally explains, this is to let customers know what they can order if not inspect inside. It would quite simply be beyond the owner's means to carry such an expensive level of stock, so the staff stand by with a warm welcome and an armful of catalogues and order forms. It seems an unusual arrangement to someone from a must-have-it-now society, but I suppose it is not that different from any Argos outlet. The main difference being your coffee table or television will take a few days rather than a few minutes to arrive.

~

Ivan Vazov is a famous son of Berkovitsa, and another

stern-looking bloke with a Stalin-sized walrus moustache. He was a poet, novelist and playwright and is often referred to as the patriarch of Bulgarian literature. His 1839 novel *Under the Yoke* is about the Ottoman oppression of Bulgaria, and has been translated into thirty languages and read by millions, including me.

Though Berkovitsa has claimed him, the great man was born elsewhere and there are monuments to him across the country. He is buried in Sofia and his home there is a museum which, the brochure confirms, contains the stuffed remains of his dog.

Vazov served as a magistrate in Berkovitsa for a year from 1879 and his house here has been immaculately restored and maintained. It was built in the National Revival style in 1815 and is a far, far cry from the drab blocks and distressed properties around the town. It is a square-ish, two story building with red tiled, gently pitched roof and dazzling white exterior. Outside, its clean lines are a delight, and inside it has not been museumified. Unusually, you really do feel you are visiting the home of someone who has just popped out for a moment.

Having done the tour and marvelled at the intricately carved Turkish wooden ceilings and strange troglodyte-style bathroom, we are seated next door at a delightful restaurant. It too has the same feel of coolness and light and openness. There is a central courtyard, with a small stream running through it, and seating under cloisters-style roofing on three sides. It is an elegant, upmarket place, and the decor and stream alone would put at least a tenner a head on the bill anywhere in Britain.

Another bonus is that the waitresses are young, pretty and very friendly. Apart from the giants with no necks, the Berkovitsans are not noticeably eastern European, or at least the average western European's idea of what eastern Europeans should look like. The girls serving us are dark with pale skins, superb bone structure and have a sort-of Celtic-ish look. Except for the language and architecture and weather and the friendliness of the staff, we could be in Bangor rather than the Balkans.

Something else I have already noted is how hard the shop and bar owners and their staff work at giving good service. It may be that the whole town has been on a customer service course, or that the Bulgarian disposition is naturally sunny and obliging. I prefer to think that in such a hard-pressed economy, the need to look after customers is more keenly felt.

It may be a coincidence, but France is the most visited country in the world and there is certainly nowhere I have been where shopkeepers seem less concerned about whether you are going to spend your money with them. Or where there are so many waiters who obviously feel superior to you just because they can fold a napkin to look like a water-lily.

The meal we had at the restaurant in Berkovitsa was as good as it was almost jaw-droppingly cheap. Under Bulgarian catering law we were obliged to start with a Shopska salad, but this one was poshed up with the addition of various peppers and spices. We then had another firm favourite, which tasted much, much better than it sounds:

Схембе Чорба
Skhembe Chorba
(Tripe Soup)

Ingredients

One lamb tripe (ask your butcher)
Six spring onions/scallions
A tablespoon of flour
Four tablespoons of butter
A teaspoon of paprika

Two eggs
Two tablespoons of vinegar
Four cloves of crushed garlic

Method

1. Wash the tripe thoroughly and put in a pot with half a dozen cups of water
2. Boil until tender, leave to cool and then chop the tripe into small pieces, preserving the stock
3. Sauté the chopped onion in the butter, add the paprika and flour and cook for several minutes
4. Add this mixture to the strained stock and bring to the boil
5. Add the tripe and season to taste
6. Boil for ten minutes, then remove from heat
7. 'Settle' the soup with the well-beaten eggs and add the vinegar
8. Serve with the crushed garlic and some hot peppers

For mains, we stayed rural and shared a huge cow's tongue and a fried pig's ear, both of which - like the tripe soup - tasted much better than you might be expected to expect. We also had some delicious stuffed vine leaves, cooked and served as follows. If you don't like the idea of eating veal you can use all pork meat, and if you are fresh out of vine leaves you can use cabbage leaves:

Сърми

Surmi

(stuffed vine leaves)

Ingredients

500g of minced veal
300g minced pork
A bunch of spring onions
Half a cup of long grain rice
A cup of yogurt
20 or so vine or cabbage leaves
100g butter
Some parsley
Some mint
Some paprika
Some pepper
Seasoning

Method

1. Sauté the finely chopped onions in some of the butter and a little water, stir in some paprika then take off the stove
2. Add the meat, the rice, pepper, mint and finely chopped parsley
3. Pour over some warm, salted water and simmer until the water has been absorbed by the rice
4. Dip vine or cabbage leaves in some hot, salted water and put a teaspoon of the mixture on each leaf
5. Roll the leaves to make a package and arrange in a saucepan
6. Pour over half a cup or so of water and some butter, put a lid on the pan and simmer gently
7. Mix the yogurt with the paprika and some melted butter and pour over

For pudding we could have had any number of sticky sweet treats but I wanted to try the famed Bulgarian doughnuts. You should be warned that this delicious confectionery should not be confused with the western street slang term for a very specific and messy sexual practice:

Мекици
Mekitsi
(Bulgarian doughnuts)

Ingredients

1 kg flour
Three eggs
500g yogurt
10g yeast
1 cup of water
Some salt
1 cup sunflower oil

Method

1. Beat the eggs, flour and yogurt together with the yeast
2. Make a soft dough and leave to stand for an hour
3. Roll the dough into a sheet and cut out circles with a tea cup
4. Deep fry and serve with icing sugar, jam, honey or of course, cheese

Среща на г-н Биг
Meeting Mr Big

Kom sits in full pomp and razor-sharp clarity, blue-green and surrounded by an ocean of blue. Snow lingers on the crest and I think how the mountain could be likened to a monstrous foam-topped wave in the instant before it crashes down and engulfs the valley. I shake my head and wonder if my dreadful simile is a result of the oxygen-enriched air, or too much pig's ear and *Rakia* yesterday.

I am feeling a little nervous as I am taking the Lada out for my first solo flight, and will limit my adventuring to a trip to Berkovitsa and the market. As Richard said, I now know the route and have seen what the standard of driving is like. I have had a crash course - if that is the right expression - in how to handle the Lada's eccentricities, and there are many.

I have seen and been coached in how windows are opened with nails, and access to the gas tank in the boot is achieved by a sharp tug on a piece of wire hanging from the roof. I should allow plenty of time and distance for stopping, and the hand brake is not in action. There is, Richard admits, considerable play in the steering, but the car is in overall good shape and sailed through its equivalent of the MOT test recently. There is, though, one final and very dread caution. Whatever the circumstances, it is imperative that I do not select fifth gear. If he knows why, Richard does not say, and the lack of explanation makes the likely penalty grow in imagined severity.

~

It is a beautiful morning, and the hills really are alive with a symphony of new life. The fruit trees lining the lane are in late blossom or heavy with free fruit. Sally says the villagers use lime tree flowers to make tea, and the sharp aroma scents the air. Wild flowers bedeck the verges, and birds squabble over the most desirable nesting places. In the distance a brace of cocks compete to make the loudest boasts of their virility, and small dogs bark just to show they can. Birds swoop and wheel overhead, and exotically named butterflies like Sooty Copper, Swallowtail and Oriental Marbled Skipper roam freely near and far.

In the midst of all this life and fecundity, there are poignant reminders that Krasiva is literally a dying village.

Because of the condition of most of the houses, it is not always easy to tell if they are occupied. But where empty houses elsewhere in Europe often bear For Sale signs, here they are marked out by photographs of the dead people who once lived in them.

Wired or taped to at least a dozen gates on my route are A4-sized posters, protected by plastic envelopes and bearing a black and white photograph of an elderly person. Curiously, all look at the camera with serious and sometimes sad expressions. This makes me wonder if they look like this because they were unused to being photographed, or the photographs were taken specifically for the purpose of display after death.

Most of the photographs are of women, but occasionally there are two posters, side by side, showing a couple now re-united in death. Some of the notices have large bows of black crepe attached to the gate, and copies have been attached to boles of trees and power cable posts on either side of the lane.

Sally Moore says that the tradition is that relatives of the deceased visit their former homes each month and distribute food to neighbours. This practice may continue indefinitely, and the photographs remain where they are until they, like their subjects, finally decompose.

As I walk through the avenue of the dead, their faces seem to look on dispassionately, and the very simplicity of this way of marking a passing makes a striking *memento mori* of how all life must end.

~

A nasty cracking sound pre-empts a shower of glass spraying through the open offside window of the Lada. I stop and instinctively try to look into the wing mirror that is no longer there. I have been driving in Bulgaria for less than five minutes and have already had a moving vehicle accident.

When I lived in rural France, confrontations in narrow lanes were so common that drivers rarely bothered to stop when wing mirrors met and damage was done. Ironically, in twenty years of driving the distance to the moon in that country, I and my cars had many near-misses, several scrapes and legions or dents but never lost a wing mirror.

Turning round in the seat, I see that my assailant has stopped twenty yards along the lane. The car is a fairly pristine right-hand drive Range Rover, but with Bulgarian plates. I get out, reaching for my phrase book and wondering if it will contain the formally correct way of saying 'You stupid bastard, what were you doing on my side of the road?'

Standing beside the Lada, I pointedly look at where my nearside wheels are within a foot of the verge, then even more pointedly pace the distance from my defunct wing mirror to the opposite verge. This is to demonstrate to the other driver that he had plenty of clearance to play with, so the damage is his responsibility.

As I take my last pace, the sun is blotted out. I turn and have to crick my neck to look up and make eye contact with a giant who would make Shrek look like a victim of last-stage anorexia.

The man who took out my wing mirror is, like the BFGs in Berkovitsa, lacking a neck, but doesn't need one to tower over me. He also does not look particularly friendly.

Like me, the man-monster is wearing the standard summer rig of short shorts, singlet and sandals, but his outfit stretches and strains in different places. Even his shaven head seems to have muscles, and his cheekbones and beetle brows are so pronounced it is hard to see if he has any eyes. In curious contrast to everything else about him, his ears and nose are neat and small. I cannot see if his teeth are bared, as he is sporting a moustache which would put the biggest, baddest walrus to shame.

I look at my phrase book, but before I can start leafing through it for the correct way of saying 'All my fault - can I pay for any damage to your car?' his moustache twitches and he speaks one, rumbling deep-bellied word:

'Problem?'

I look at his biceps and then at the shattered wing mirror, then swallow, smile a sick smile and mutter in a near-falsetto voice:

'No problem.'

He continues to look down on me thoughtfully, then turns and strides back to his car. I pick up pieces of glass and wonder how I am going to explain to Richard that his beloved Lada has been attacked by a Big and potentially Very Unfriendly Giant.

~

I have reached Berkovitsa with no further incident, but that was only because I sneaked in behind a giant farm machine being transported on a low loader and escorted by two vans with flashing lights. I don't think the driver of the vehicle at the rear appreciated me putting myself in between him and the combine harvester, but I took no notice of his flashing lights and hooter.

Now I am looking for a parking spot, and Berkovitsa seems full. I join a queue behind what looks like a golf buggy, which is itself shadowing a Cold War-era lorry laden with wood. They are both following a coffin-cart pulled by a smartly turned-out trotting pony. A family of Roma is aboard, and seem to have dressed up for market day. The older of the two women looks particularly impressive and puts me in mind of the illustrations outside tents at travelling fairs in the 1950's. The posters promised that The Original Gypsy Lee was waiting inside to reveal what Fate held in store for you. She must have been a very busy and fast-moving fortune-teller, as she appeared at different fairgrounds and travelling shows all across the country, often at the same time. The illustrations always showed a dark-featured lady in heavily brocaded top and a colourful headscarf fringed with gold coins, and that is exactly what this lady is wearing.

It would be interesting to discover how traditional this costume is, and how it has changed since the Roma left northern India 1,500 years ago. From there they stayed in or migrated through the Balkans to arrive in medieval Europe around a millennium ago. Now it is estimated that there are twelve million Roma worldwide and around

400,000 live in Bulgaria. Over the centuries they have faced horrific persecution, and two million were believed to have been amongst the first to die in Hitler's concentration camps.

Absorbed with the Roma family, I follow the golf buggy and the lorry as they turn off and go down a side street leading to the square. They both pull up outside an official-looking building, and I am left stranded on the edge of the square. I can't reverse as another lorry has pulled up behind me, so drive into the square and out of it at the earliest opportunity. I am not unaware that the town police station is on the nearest corner, and that on-duty officers like to gather at the kiosk outside. As I speed by, a heavily-set policeman regards me thoughtfully, then hitches up his trousers and turns back to his coffee and cigarette.

~

Over the years, I have found that all street markets share some similarities, but vary from town to town as well as country to country.

Here at Berkovitsa, the similarities include rows of stalls and the enthusiasm of the shoppers; the dissimilarities include the size of the vegetables and fruit on sale, and the silence of the stallholders.

In England they would be advertising their wares by shouting in special market traders' patois. In the Middle East you would be lucky to get by without being accosted and talked into buying a carpet. Here, the vendors stand silently in front of their piles of potatoes, huge bunches of spring onions and garlic, politely waiting for the customers to place an order. To be fair, the fruit and vegetables do sell themselves, and the tomatoes are the biggest and juiciest-looking I have ever seen.

It is a covered market in the centre of the shopping area, and the owners of the surrounding businesses have taken advantage of the dramatic increase in passing trade by moving their stock on to the pavement. Boxes of shoes, garden implements and even bread and cakes jostle for attention, and I stop to buy a hunting knife. I don't need or want a hunting knife and anyway won't be able to take it on to the plane when I leave, but such is the lure of getting something for a fraction of what it would have cost at home.

Interestingly for such a poor area of a poor country, there is an absence of buskers, street entertainers or straightforward beggars. At the weekly street market where I live in Hampshire, shoppers have to run a bizarre gauntlet of four musicians playing accordion, guitar, saxophone and harmonica. It is a bizarre experience because they are individual acts, and each playing a different tune. Then there will be Big Issue salespeople, a man pretending to be a statue, and a man with a dog, slumped against a wall and either too far gone or too embarrassed to thank people who drop a coin into the dog's bowl.

The only person on the floor of this market is the Roma lady I saw earlier. She sits, legs daintily out to one side and resting one hand on the ground, and is completely encircled by concentric rings of candles. At first I think she must be offering some sort of fortune telling or supernatural service, then realise the candles are not props, but for sale. They are too small to be any use at home except on birthday cakes, so I assume they must be for visits to church. Now and then a passer-by will stop, reach down, give her a coin and receive a candle. I stand and watch and notice she never smiles or thanks her customers, and her face remains completely unchanged in expression. It is a very beautiful face in spite of her advanced years, and her eyes are huge, but like her face, expressionless.

I step forward and show her my camera and ask with gestures if it is okay to take her photograph. She gives an almost imperceptible nod and her expression does not alter as she looks incuriously into the lens. After decades of photographing people for publicity stunts or to accompany magazine articles, it is a strange experience for me to look through the viewfinder at someone who is so clearly unconcerned with how the camera will see her.

Not wanting to appear patronising, I nod my thanks and take the candles she proffers when I press a couple of screwed-up, high denomination notes into her hand. Before I turn away I think about showing her the images I have captured, then realise how stupid I am being. I think that she, like the subjects of the death notices in the village, will have little interest in how people who see her image will perceive her.

~

We have pound shops a-plenty in Britain, so it should follow that Bulgaria has its lev shops. But it still comes as a surprise to see a store where you can buy a tennis racquet or a brassiere for around forty pence.

I have to negotiate a large dog lying across the entrance, but he is well-fed and shows little interest as I step over him. He has no collar, so is probably an official street dog. It is particularly pleasing to know that though he will have no single owner, the whole town will be taking responsibility for him.

Unwanted dogs are a huge problem throughout Eastern Europe, and horror stories about their callous treatment and disposal are legion. In Bulgaria, thousands of dedicated individuals and charities work tirelessly to rescue dogs and cats and send them to welcoming homes in other countries.

But some authorities here take a very practical yet eminently humane approach. Together with other EU member states, Bulgaria strictly prohibits the killing of strays. Instead, they must be rounded up, neutered and then offered for adoption. If not found a home, they are released where they were caught. This may sound callous, but there is an onus on municipal mayors to provide facilities for strays. And it is clear that the people are happy to take a share in providing for the cats and dogs that live on the streets. I think you can tell a lot about a country or at least its aspirations by the way it treats its domestic animals. Of course there will be mindless cruelty and neglect here as elsewhere, but at least Bulgaria is trying to manage the problem.

Having paid the guard dog the entrance fee of a bit of my kebab, I enter and pick up a can of shaving foam, some washing-up liquid and a potato peeler without a problem. I also pick up a thermometer so I can check if it is as hot as it seems. But then I want something I can't see, so it's time to go into Marcel Marceau mode.

We all have different techniques for asking for what we want in shops in countries where we do not speak the language. I once watched in dumbstruck admiration in a French bar as a British customer successfully ordered a round of drinks and a meal by constantly repeating 'bonjour' as he pointed at beer pumps and bottles and items on the menu. I have a friend who takes an even more creative approach to language communication barriers. Wherever she is in the world, she will speak in English, but with a really over-the-top version of the pronunciation and accent we associate with that country. So when in Germany, she sounds like Marlene Dietrich lampooning herself in English. My friend believes this technique helps the person she is talking to understand what she is saying; amazingly it often seems to.

But speaking in mime requires a whole set of skills at different levels. Anyone can point at an item on the menu or mimic a wing-flapping, squawking hen when seeking eggs in a grocery shop. But it can take a high level of inventiveness and even real talent to enquire about more obscure items.

My first circle of the shop with arms straight out from my shoulders as I buzzed loudly and tried to look bug-eyed did nothing for the three young lady assistants. They look completely unfazed, so I suppose it is not unusual for the shop to be taken over by a mad foreigner doing what small children do when pretending they can fly. One actually took photos with her phone, while another went out into the street to invite passers-by to join the fun. Even the old dog roused itself and came in to see what all the fuss was about.

Now I have quite an audience, and the suggestions are coming in thick and fast. A model airplane kit and a child's Superman pyjama set have been produced and rejected, and one of the passers-by has for some inexplicable reason suggested an egg-timer. Then, as I run into an invisible barrier, adopt a horrified expression and do a tail-spin to the floor, someone gets it. The girl who has been filming me for inclusion in the Bulgarian version of You Tube suddenly snaps her fingers, runs to a shelf and returns with a fly-swatter. There is a rippling of applause till I make a see-sawing 'close but no cigar' motion. I take the swatter, then hold up a finger for attention and pretend to be trying to free myself from a glutinous morass.

A great sigh of mutual comprehension goes round the store, and the girl says something like 'mockolovka'.

At least they now all know that I am after flypaper, even though the shop does not stock it.

~

A little later and I am where the customers in the lev store agree will be my best bet to find flypaper. It is a very traditional-style hardware store, and sitting behind the counter amongst a riot of pots and pans and household implements hanging from the ceiling is an elderly lady.

I did not see her at first as it is dark in the shop and she is as still as a roadside honey seller. But she is smiling at me, so is hopefully alive and awake. When my attempts to reproduce the word the woman in the lev shop used, the lady actually looks as if she gets it, continues to smile, and then nods her head as if humouring me. She makes no move, so in case she did not understand, I go into mime mode and do a circuit of the shop before finishing with the dying fly routine.

Again, she smiles and nods her head but remains unmoved. We are at stalemate.

Then a door behind the counter opens, and a middle-aged man looks in to see what is going on. I repeat my attempt at saying 'flypaper' and launch into the mime routine for good measure. He looks at me as if I am mad, then nods his head brusquely, turns and walks back through the doorway. Long minutes pass as I stand, inanely responding to the old lady's smile and nods. Eventually, the door opens again and the man returns. I note he is empty handed and looking even more irritated, so I thank him and his mother and leave.

It is only as I reach the pavement that I remember the basic caution every guide book to Bulgaria stresses. In this country, shaking the head is a positive response, while nodding is a negative, as in 'Yes, we have no flypaper...'

~

If asking for what I want was a problem in the lev shop, it is going to be even more so in grocery stores.

It's fine with easily recognisable items like fruit and veg in the raw, but not with cans or jars bearing no illustration or other visual clue. I recently heard Des O'Connor telling a story on television about how he spent a week in Spain eating cat food because he could not read the label and assumed the tin contained tuna. Funnily enough, he said, he developed quite a taste for it. At the time I thought he was making a gag, but I can now see how that could happen.

According to the *Daily Telegraph*, humans across the planet may actually be speaking the same language without realising it. The report says that scientists have found that the words used to describe common objects and ideas can be strikingly similar. As an example they say that the word for 'nose' is likely to include the sounds 'neh' or 'ooh'

So far so good, as Bulgarian for 'nose' is 'nos', but other commonalities are few and far between. Fortunately and for some reason, some words from other languages have come into common usage. The word for 'thank you' is Благодаря, which comes out something like *blagodaryah*, but the French *merci* is common currency. Also, 'goodbye' sounds like *do-veezh-da-ne*, but many younger people prefer the Italian *ciao*, which - as in Rome and elsewhere - can mean either 'hi' or 'see you later'.

Actually and going on my limited experiences, I reckon Bulgarian will not be as difficult to learn as other closer-to-home languages. This is because, when speaking a foreign language in its home country, you are usually required to not only say the right word, but *say it in the approved way*. In France, this is particularly true. This is partly because pronunciation and delivery is important in their language, but also because they do not like foreigners and particularly British foreigners trifling with their language. I have lost count of how often a Frenchman has looked at me in mystified horror when I have said something really basic, then, when he has tired of the game, repeated it in exactly the same way as I said it. This does not seem to happen here, perhaps because there are no fancy-dan rules of intonation, pitch, stress and pronunciation. Proof of this is that you generally know from a good distance when people are speaking a foreign language. You may not be able to hear the words, but you can tell if they are speaking French, Italian or Dutch just by the flow and sound of the conversation. Not so with Bulgarian, and I constantly assume I am nearing a group speaking English when they are in fact talking in their native tongue. For me, though, the problem is not the need for getting the pronunciation right, but of knowing so little of the language. This is of course, further complicated when the label on the can says котешка храна and there is no picture of a contented cat to give you a clue to what is inside.

Luckily for me, one of the assistants in the convenience store I have found speaks a little French, another is fluent in Italian, and the other is very good at interpreting mime. Consequently, I am on my way back to Krasiva with a bottle of good Scotch for my host at dinner this evening and hopefully, not a single tin of Bulgarian Kit-e-Kat.

~

It seems I was right not to challenge the wing-mirror assassin and demand compensation. The big man with the big moustache is in fact a local Mr Big in more ways than one.

According to Ivalin - who somehow knew about the incident and confrontation almost before it happened - the giant is one of a family with a long history in the area.

They rear lambs in a very modern farm building outside the village, then slaughter and sell them through their own butchery shop in Berkovitsa. The shop is below a block of flats also owned by the family.

Although I am sure it is only local gossip, it is further alleged that another enterprise run by the family is money-lending. Many Bulgarians are fanatical gamblers, and it is said that the family will loan money to fund any level of habit. If the borrowers do not pay the principle and the interest back it is also said they will find themselves approached by Mr Big. Although it is probably not true I can see that not many normal-sized Bulgarians would want to find themselves in debt to Mr Big and his family.

We are at dinner at Ivalin's home, which is at the very extremes of the village. Beyond his garden lies the valley, and the very off-road route to his secret strawberry and raspberry fields.

I arrived to find him sitting with two men in what looks like a rustic bus shelter alongside the track. It obviously serves the function of the Women's Institute hut in Krasiva, and provides a meeting place for villagers to sit and talk and watch the world go by. Or to be strictly accurate, not go by. One of the men looks quite worryingly like a miniature version of me, with tousled grey hair and beard and a much smaller and less-abused snub nose. The other is the man-child I met outside the guest house, and he is still wearing his Soviet officer's hat and carrying his fruit-picking bottle-on-a-stick. I now know that his name is Kratzi, and he suffers from schizophrenia and alcoholism. Nobody knows where the officer's hat came from, but the villagers keep him supplied with clothes. Ivalin supplies his lodgings, which are in a barn next to the main house.

Also attending the meeting was Ivalin's donkey, which lives in a stable beside the barn, and his clearly devoted cross-collie called Johnny.

The sun is setting over a distant range of hills, and the air is sweetened by the wildflowers Ivalin has nurtured in his garden. My host has produced a bottle of raspberry *Rakia* made from some of the fruit not despatched to the jam-making factory in Sofia which is his main customer. I have brought a case of cold beer and a bottle of Scotch whisky. Bulgaria produces its own whisky, but as Ivalin says, it is nothing like the real thing. He knows about my

Scottish ancestry and has already proposed a twinning of Aberdeen and the nearby Balkan town of Gabravo. The alleged meanness of the burghers is legendary, and it is said that you can always tell a dog from Gabravo through its lack of tail. It is not that docking is a local custom, but the accidents caused by Gabravoans shutting their doors so quickly to keep the heat in during the long, hard winters.

~

The Balkans loom against a velvet sky, and an owl mournfully seeks a mate.

I am in a rocking chair on the roof, savouring the cool night air and a final tot of Ivalin's raspberry *Rakia*. This evening I learned more about him and what a remarkable man he is. As well as a soft-fruit entrepreneur and local historian, he is a degree-holding engineer and a mountaineer of repute. He is the only man in the area known to have crossed the valley and ascended Kom in the depths of winter, wearing a customised set of ski-shoes of his own contrivance.

He also seems to have a network of contacts and informants of which the KGB would have been proud, and we had a curious conversation towards the end of the evening. To get the full flavour, you will need to imagine me speaking with a slur, and he giving his uncanny impression of the talking meerkat:

He: 'You hev been a bed men.'

Me: 'Oh? Excuse me, but I think you will find it was your donkey that just farted, not me.'

He: 'I mean you hev been driving in a forbidden street in Berkovitsa, and afterwards in the square.'

Me: 'But I only followed some cars down the street, then I had to go through the square to get out of it.'

He: 'The cars you followed were...authorised.'

Me: 'Oh. Okay. How did you know about my forbidden activity?'

He: 'I heard from a friend who heard from the police. They recognised the car and called him.'

Me: 'You mean they called Richard?'

He: 'No. They spoke to my friend and he called me.'

Me: 'Ah. So what happens next?'

He: 'Nothing. The police know you are a foreigner and my friend asked them to do nothing. You will be lucky this time.'

Me: 'I see. And who is your friend?'

He: 'You will meet him soon.'

Me: 'Ah. And is that how things are done in Bulgaria?'

He: 'Sometimes.'

Me: 'Right-o. Cheers, then.'

He: '*Nazdrave*...'

At dinner with Ivalin I was introduced to other varieties of fruit-flavoured *Rakia*, and some interesting dishes. We started with the almost compulsory shopska salad, accompanied with home-made Tutmanik cheese bread and green fig preserve, which could be taken as a jam or relish. Incidentally the scientists claiming that most languages use similar sounds would be pleased to note how alike the Bulgarian 'konfityur' and the French 'confiture' are when jam is being discussed in those countries. Like many villagers, Ivalin's garden has a fine fig tree, and this is his very simple recipe:

Конфитюр зелена смокиня
Konfityur zelena smokinya
(green fig jam)

Ingredients

A kg of plump green figs*
500g sugar
5g citric acid

Method

1. Cut the stems off the figs, level with the fruit
2. Pierce the fruit all over
3. Boil in a pan of water for five minutes
4. Change the water and boil the fruit for another five minutes
5. Repeat the process (this is to remove bitterness and to soften the fruit)
6. Make a syrup of 100g of the sugar and 300g water and boil for 15 minutes to further soften the fruit
7. Add another 400g of sugar and re-boil

8. Next day, re-boil until the mixture is of the right consistency
9. Before removing from the heat, add 5g citric acid to avoid crystallisation
10. Remove foam and put into sterilised, dry glass containers. Seal and store in a dark and cool place

N.B. *This is the jam recipe. To make a chutney, you just need to add onions and seasoning, brown sugar, ginger and some other fruit for bulking-out, such as apricots or sultanas. Experimenting is part of the fun.*

By the way, figs *come in different colours and 'green' does not mean unripe. All figs grow straight out from the stem and then droop as gravity comes into play.*

As far as I can discover, *hotchpotch* and *gyuvetch* are the pots this sort of dish is cooked in, and as with *balti* in Indian cooking, have become the names of this type of cooking in the oven. Or the other way around, and the pots were named for the dishes cooked in them. Wherever it comes from, the Oxford Dictionary defines 'hotchpotch' as a confused mixture, coming from the Late Middle English term for a mutton stew. Bulgarian *hotchpotch* is said to have originated at the Rila monastery* some centuries ago, and the monastery has long been in the forefront of the mission to keep traditional Bulgarian cuisine alive and well.

Манастир Гювеч
Monastery Gyuvetch
(hotchpotch stew)

Ingredients

A kilo of beef
4 chopped tomatoes
250g mushrooms
A cup of long-grain rice
A chopped onion
A dozen olives
1 tbsp butter
2 tbsp olive oil
A tbsp sugar
Two cups beef stock
Some paprika
Some seasoning

Method

1. Cut the beef into small pieces and fry in oil in a suitable oven-proof pot for five or so minutes Add the onion, paprika and beef stock
2. After five minutes, add the mushrooms
3. After another five minutes, add the tomatoes, butter, sugar and olives and salt to taste and cook for a further five minutes
4. Put the pot into a preheated oven at 200°C and cook for half an hour or so

*Founded by a 10th-century hermit and set in the highest mountain in the Balkans seventy miles south of Sofia, Rila Monastery is one of the nine UNESCO World Heritage sites in Bulgaria, and features on the one lev banknote. I have never actually met a one lev banknote in person, but must assume there are millions alive and well in Bulgaria

Пържени филийки
Purzheni filiiki
(French toast)

It is an interesting etymological fact how such a simple dish can have such a lot of history. When I was young, French toast was a slice of bread which had been toasted on one side only. I don't know why, but it was probably an insult to our oldest enemies and suggested they could not even make toast properly. Elsewhere, it has long meant bread which has been dipped into egg and milk and fried. Apparently, French toast is not in fact French in origin, but was invented in 5th century Rome and served with honey as *pan dulcis*. In 15th century France, *pain perdu* or 'lost bread' was a popular recipe for using up stale bread by dipping it in egg and milk. Now it gets really complicated, as the originator of the modern term is believed to be an 18th century New York innkeeper. His name, so the story goes, was Joseph French, and he advertised the tasty snack as 'French Toast' because he was challenged in the possessive apostrophe department.

Whatever the origin of the dish and its name, *Purzheni filiiki* is Bulgarian for 'French toast' and they like it done this way as a sweet or savoury dish:

Ingredients

Some stale bread
Three eggs
A cupful of milk
Some vegetable oil

Method

1. Slice the bread thinly Dip them first into the milk, then into the beaten eggs
2. Fry
3. Serve piping hot, with sugar, honey, jam or cheese topping - or all at the same time (Elenko likes his *à la Elvis* with mashed banana on top)

Да останеш местно
Staying local

Hot, hot, hot.

Yesterday I left the lev shop thermometer in the full sun, and it exploded. I looked at the scale before throwing it away and saw it only went up to 50C.

Kom has lost his capping of snow, yet despite the heat and lack of rain the valley is still verdantly green. Cows and goats graze contentedly on the lush pastureland, and distant figures in straw hats watch over their animals or work amongst beehives and vines. From a purely mercenary perspective, the view from my window would be valued in millions in a posh part of Switzerland. Here it comes with a house valued at the equivalent of a few thousand pounds.

The media has begun to call Bulgaria the 'new Spain' but few would-be expats in Britain seems to be taking notice of the incentives of wonderful weather, sometimes incredibly cheap property prices, a low cost of living and some really friendly locals.

I am taking the sun and enjoying a breakfast tub of yogurt, left on the doorstep with a bottle of his equally home-made wine by Elenko. The yogurt is delicious but I will save the wine for cooking or treating insect bites.

Life is good, but there is a small problem I must address, and it may take my moving house or committing murder to solve.

I am second to nobody in my affection for dogs and grew up with a houseful of them, as did my children. But they were urban dogs and took their townie characteristics and behaviour with them wherever we lived. Basically, from their perspective they were there to be indulged in return for unlimited, totally over-the-top and probably feigned loyalty and affection.

To anyone who has lived in the countryside, it is clear that rural dogs have an entirely different take on their roles and responsibilities.

Urban dogs are generally streetwise and calculating, and know how they are expected to act to win food, lodgings and love. They also like to sleep at night.

Country dogs seem naturally contrary, and both naive and indifferent at the same time. They lay in the road expecting cars to drive round them and cannot be bothered to be nice to their owners. To be fair, this lack of demonstrated affection can be mutual.

One common and constant trait of all country dogs is that they are universally hostile to strangers. I suppose they would argue that this is a main part of their job, but the problem is that they don't know when to stop. In towns, things are different. Dogs do not generally kick up such as fuss about a stranger passing by as this is not exactly a novelty.

Things are understandably different in a small village or hamlet, and if a dog is tied up in a yard all day it must come as a welcome break to have something to make a fuss about. The standard accepted rules of engagement are that the village dog will bark at the stranger until he has moved on and is no longer a threat. Then it will stop barking.

This is clearly not the case in Bulgaria, or at least not in the village of Krasiva, and I think I know part of the reason.

I once had to spend a week in the geriatric ward of a big hospital. This was not solely because of my age or mental condition, but because of a shortage of beds. The nurses on day shift would allow or even encourage the patients to sleep all day, and it was the night staff and we patients who had to put up with all the groaning and moaning and calls for attention.

It is almost exactly the same situation here. All the dogs spend their days snoozing in the sun and remain silent, then make up for it during the night. This is not because of a prevalence of burglars, foxes, wolves or bears passing by, but because they are wide awake and probably bored. What the dogs of Krasiva are doing is barking purely for barking's sake. Either that or they are having long-distance conversations to while away the night-time hours.

There is clearly a pecking order, and the top dog lives next door. I do not know the name of Madame Tzvetana's mongrel or even if he has one, but he is always the catalyst. It may be that he needs to see a canine psychiatrist because of sleep apnea problems or constant nightmares, but every hour he will kick off with a series of growls and yelps which end in a crescendo of frantic barking. This will be the signal for the two dogs who live opposite and the three on the same side of the road to join in. Then will come a deep and distant but highly penetrating howling from somewhere in the valley below. The night chorus will go on for five minutes or so, then tail off and silence will return. Sometimes the dog next door will not sound off for an hour or so; sometimes it will be within minutes, and the not knowing is part of the torture.

I cannot ask Madam if she could keep her dog inside at night as I do not know the language and doubt she would understand the concept of a dog ever entering the house.

Ivalin does not seem to grasp the problem, and I think he and the other villagers have become so used to the night-time concerto that they don't notice it. Maybe if it stopped they would find it hard to sleep.

Something will have to be done, even if it means buying some really dodgy meat from the processing factory at Komerinski.

~

I am on my way to the local shop, and see that the weather has brought the villagers out to play. Old Mother Russia acknowledges me with a dignified nod from the shady bench opposite her home, and other residents and visiting relatives work in gardens or the family vineyards which line the upper hills. Several villagers are harvesting green figs from the communal tree in the garden of a big, empty house. It used to belong to the mayor, so I suspect they take special pleasure in helping themselves.

Further along the lane, a sleek pony stands looking down its nose at old Ivan's donkey and cart as the chauffeur of a limousine might look at the driver of an inferior car. The pony is attached to a Roma cart, and its owners are stripping mulberries from one of the trees lining the verge. They are technically on public land, so there will be no objection from the villagers even if they are not happy to see free food being harvested for profit. They know the Roma will empty the trees and sell what they cannot eat for pennies by the side of a main road or at Berkovitsa market. It may not please the locals, but to me it seems selling such an abundance of natural produce must be better than letting it rot. Also, I think that many of the older villagers became so used to communism that they find small examples of private enterprise somehow distasteful. This may be another reason the Roma are not universally popular in Bulgaria.

~

I do not know who shears Elenko's sheep, but it looks as if the same person has been let loose on his hair. His bare head sprouts sporadic tufts of grey hair surrounded by lacerated pink skin. One of the worst cuts has been partially covered by two sticking plasters, arranged in the traditional x-marks-the-spot pattern favoured by comic strip artists and treasure map creators.

Elenko sees me looking and smiles ruefully, then goes into his house and returns with a smart new electric razor. It belongs, he explains with a rather good miming sequence, to Richard, and he borrowed it to give himself a trim. It ran away with him, but Sally has promised to neaten him up this afternoon before dinner.

I have stopped by to thank him for his gifts of yogurt and wine, and to drop off a return present of a couple of bananas and an orange. He likes soft fruit because of his lack of teeth, and the more exotic fruits can be comparatively expensive. Most rural Bulgarians of Elenko's age would have lost most if not all of their teeth by natural decay, but there is a story whispered in the village concerning his youthful adventures, petrol siphoning and a revolver.

We stand and mime-talk and I exhaust my Bulgarian vocabulary by observing that his *ovtsa* (sheep) look well, that it is a nice day (*khubav den*) and that Kom has lost its topping of snow (*snyag*). I tried to make a joke about the mountain and Elenko both losing their hair, but it was far beyond my verbal and miming skills.

As I indicate I am on my way to the shop, he holds up a hand, returns to the house and comes out with a dish of what looks like raw hamburgers or flattened meatballs, and a trio of bottles. I don't know if the tradition in other countries applies here, but every time I give something to Elenko, he returns the compliment. Now we have established a never-ending exchange, like a friendly vendetta with tit-for-tat presents rather than killings.

I don't know what is on the dish, but I can tell that one of the bottles contains his home-made wine. The small bottle is filled with the innocent-looking colourless liquid which must be *Rakia*. The other is a plastic *Coca-Cola* bottle half-filled with a viscous liquid. Elenko obviously wants me to toast the morning with him and holds out the cola bottle.

It is a little early for me, but I do not want to seem rude, so take it, nod my thanks, unscrew the cap and lift the bottle to my lips. Before I swallow too much, he snatches the bottle away, wags a reproving finger and points at the sky. After he slaps himself around the face and shoulders a couple of times, I realise that the bottle contains not one of his home made beverages, but some sort of sun blocker. He hands me a glass of wine to take the taste away, so I am able to blame my wincing and pained expression on having imbibed the sun-tan lotion.

I wave as I pat Chiro the donkey and walk away, and Elenko toasts me with the *Rakia* bottle as he returns to his tumbledown cottage. It would be patronising to say he is a simple man and happy with what he has got, but he is certainly no less happy than many people I know with big houses and cars, mortgages and overdrafts. It is early days yet, and I am still wearing the rose-tinted glasses of the typical visitor to a less-privileged society. But I have to wonder if my friend would be any happier in a draught-free, centrally-heated, warden-controlled care home apartment in Britain rather than with his animals in this poor but familiar little village.

~

Approaching the square I hear some blood-curdling squeals coming through an open window. I stop and listen and realise it is not a pig or spouse being slaughtered, but the sound of a radio playing a traditional Bulgarian air.

It is hard to describe the folk music of the region and country, but it seems to be a strange hybrid. There is a typically hypnotic Middle Eastern cadence and rhythm, but it is infused with the sort of blackboard-scratching wail one associates with bagpipes in Scotland or Brittany. The instruments are often accompanied by vocals familiar in tone to anyone who attended a folk club in the early Sixties.

Perhaps surprisingly, the Bulgars claim Orpheus the Greek God of music as one of their own, and that he was born in the Rhodope mountains in the 3rd century BC. It was said his airs could pacify the wildest animals and he could even charm the rocks into dancing. When Jason and his Argonauts passed the fatally attractive Sirens, it was his music that saved the crew.

The house from where the music comes is one of handful along one side of the square. The properties are mostly of the communist cubic variety, but some are mud-and wattle originals.

In one corner on the side of the square overlooking the valley is a war memorial, and alongside it what appears to be a communist monument. Both are in much better condition than the single-storey block which once held the village hall and official offices. From what can be seen through the dirty windows, the hall has not been used for a long time. Between it and the monument is an interesting example of a typical Bulgarian bus stop. It takes the form of a giant metal ladder, bent into a semi-circle and with each end planted into the floor. Below it is strung a row of girders with gaps between them, and below that is a metal framework which looks like the sort of thing you saw on the top of goon towers at checkpoints in East Germany during the Cold War.

Sitting in the shelter are Kratzi and another villager I have not yet met. He is about my age and as big as Kratzi is small, and has a large-featured face with a pair of old-fashioned spectacles on his bulbous nose. He is wearing a ball cap, a well-worn polo shirt, a pair of violently checked Bermuda shorts and trainers of the sort that pretend to be a famous and expensive brand. I did not expect the villagers to be wearing traditional Bulgarian costumes on a daily basis, but was surprised to see the mixture of older formal and modern-style dress. As I look at the pair, I realise another reason I feel so at home in Krasiva. Here, my style of dress appears positively conservative.

Kratzi explains that his companion's name is Petar and offers me a space on the bus shelter bench. At the same time he points conspiratorially at a large plastic beer bottle between his feet. I think I would enjoy passing an hour or so in company on a lovely day with a cold beer to hand, but shrug regretfully and make the signal that I am driving later.

The shop is housed in a large, red-tiled building alongside the hall and bus shelter. It is as ill-maintained as the hall, but some effort has been made to make it look inviting. The frontage has been whitewashed within the last decade, and an old tractor tyre lies on its side by the door, sprouting an attractive orange-coloured plant. More death notices are pasted on to a board on the other side of the door, which I find is locked.

I rattle the handle and am turning to walk away when I see a twitch of the vertical plastic strips acting as blinds for the window. Then comes a long drawn-out series of rattles and clanks before the door creaks open and I find myself looking up at Mr Big's mother. Or perhaps his sister or grandmother.

She is a tall, ageless woman with a haircut almost as severe as her expression. She is wearing a dark smock-type overall and I am reminded of the scene in every Hammer Horror film when Count Dracula's familiar opens the castle door to admit the next victim.

I ask with my eyebrows if the shop is open and she shakes her head, shows her small, pointed teeth in a sort of smile and opens the door wider. I step over the threshold and notice how cold it is inside despite the heat of the day. There is more rattling and clanking behind me, and I look round to see Madame re-locking the door. Then she glides past me and takes up her place behind the counter as I remember that it is only eight hour's drive from here across the border into Romania, and then on to Transylvania. Flying time must be even less.

~

I was wrong about the shop lady. She is very nice and from Berkovitsa, not Transylvania. The door was locked because the catch doesn't work and she had the blinds pulled down to discourage the sunlight. She looks very proper, but my antics broke cultural barriers as we did a re-run of the lev shop charades game. I would flap my arms and squat and cluck, and she would rush behind the counter. If she returned with eggs, we both won points. If she came back with laxative chocolate we had to start again.

Several villagers arrived during the game, pretending they had come to shop. All stayed on to join in and advise Madame on what they thought I wanted.

Eventually I had won most of the items I came for and the show was over. I suppose in a village where not much happens, any diversion is of interest.

As I leave, I look up at the sky, then the view across the valley and then to where Kratzi and Petar are sitting. Ivalin's battered white van has pulled up, and he is unloading punnets of strawberries for the shop. Further away, Elenko is approaching with his sheep and donkey. I hesitate, then return to the shop for a couple of the half-gallon bottles of beer from the cold counter, some packets of crisps, a length of sausage and a large white loaf.

I shall put my visit to town off until tomorrow. I think I may be getting in to the swing of things and the proper pace of life here, and a leisurely picnic with friends seems a pretty perfect way to spend a summer's afternoon.

As with feta-like cheese, champagne and cricket, there's an ongoing dispute about who can claim authorship of yogurt.

After five hundred years of occupation and rule, you might expect Bulgarians to share some cultural aspects with Turkey, and yogurt is one of them. The word itself is Turkish, and common in many languages in the region.

The idea of making use of fermented milk is thousands of years old, and like many great things is thought to have been discovered or invented by accident. Carrying it in containers made from animal stomachs would have curdled the milk, which is essentially what yogurt is. One notable fan was the great warlord Genghis Khan, and it is said by some that the founder of the Mogul Empire and his whole army lived almost exclusively on yogurt. Naturally, Bulgaria claims to make the best yogurt in the universe, and says the credit should go to Stamen Grigorov (1878 -1945). As well as creating anti-tuberculosis vaccine he discovered the bacillus* essential to the making of yogurt. It is said that, because of this bacillus, yogurt in its original variety can be produced only in the natural climatic conditions in Bulgaria and some neighbouring regions on the Balkan peninsula. There is a museum dedicated to yogurt in Grigorov's home village, and making this globally popular foodstuff in quantity could hardly be simpler:

Кисело мляко
Kisselo mlyako
(DIY Yogurt)

Ingredients

4 litres of milk
500g of plain yogurt with active bacteria*

Method

1. Put the milk in a large saucepan and boil
2. Put it aside and let it cool for half an hour or so (it should be warm but not hot, and an ideal temperature is 45°C)
3. Beat the yogurt in a bowl, add a little milk and mix briskly
4. Gradually add the mixture to the rest of the milk and keep mixing
5. Pour the resultant mixture into bowls or jars with lids
6. Cover with a towel or blanket to keep warm and leave for three hours
7. Uncover and let it stand for half an hour
8. Put it in the fridge.

Almost unbelievably, you can (as the advert says) remove the 'stress' of making yogurt with a machine. More sensibly, you can buy sachets of yogurt culture starter and almost guarantee success. It can also be fun to create your own flavoured yogurt by adding dollops of jams, honey, maple syrup or vanilla, lemon or even coffee extract.

The flattened meatballs Elenko gave me are hugely popular, and are eaten hot or cold and on their own, as part of a meal or in a sandwich. They have their own versions in Turkey and Greece and elsewhere in the region, and may be known as *Kufteh*, *Kofte*, *Kofta* and even *keftedes*:

кюфте
Kyufte
(meatballs)

Ingredients

A kilo of minced meat (60 percent pork and 40 percent beef is the norm)
One large onion finely chopped
A teaspoon of cumin
A clove of finely minced garlic
A tablespoon of salt
A tablespoon of black pepper

Method

1. Mix all the ingredients in a bowl and leave in fridge for half an hour
2. Make into balls and then flatten into a rough hamburger shape
3. Fry in hot oil or grill. If you want the authentic look you will need a grilling device which will leave dark stripes across your kyuftes

NB. Kyuftes are not to be confused with kebapches, which are the same but have no onions in them.

This is another very big favourite with sweet-toothed Bulgarians, and has a similar recipe but another name in Turkey, Macedonia and most Middle Eastern countries. Also known as *Balkan Talumbe*, they are not dissimilar to French *choux* pastries or Spanish *churros*:

Сладки топки тесто
Sladki topki testo
(sweet dough balls with syrup)

Ingredients

Three eggs
150g cottage (or white) cheese
A cup of all-purpose flour
A cup of sugar
A teaspoon of vanilla essence
A teaspoon of baking soda
Three cups of water
A cupful of vegetable oil

Method

1. Mix the cottage cheese and eggs
2. Gradually add the flour and then the baking soda
3. Shape into balls with a spoon and fry in hot oil
4. Make the syrup from water, sugar and vanilla and pour over

На влака
On the train

I sit in an almost spookily patient queue of cars, lorries and carts as a small man laboriously winds the large wheel which opens and shuts the railway crossing barrier on the back road into Berkovitsa.

On one corner of the junction, a couple of workmen sit outside a bar looking speculatively at their empty glasses as if considering whether to pay and go or start again. Over the road is another bar with a spectacularly distressed moped outside, and next door is a store selling new car parts. Next to that is a yard piled high with used tyres, which the owner is apparently reclaiming. He wears a grimy set of overalls and is working in a corrugated tin shed, doing something with a large hammer to a lumpy-looking lorry tyre. A breaker's yard further along the road is full of dead cars. There seem an inordinate number of car-related businesses in and around Berkovitsa. This is probably a result of the age and condition of most of the cars on the road, the insane approach to driving... or a combination of both factors.

The barrier lifted, we shuffle through and over the lines

and I park the car next to the breaker's yard. I get half way across the road before returning to move it. Even in Berkovitsa the Lada looks past its sell-by date, and I don't want the owners of the yard thinking it has been left for them.

Amongst the bland, post-war buildings, the railway station is a thing of comparative beauty. Its clean, angular lines and pitched roof suggest a neo-classical approach and contrast nicely with the ornately arched windows and doors. They are freshly-painted in white and the building itself is a strong shade of magnolia. Signs of a previous era include what looks like a goon tower alongside the platform, and a large star-shaped recess above the main door. There is another, smaller star on a commemorative plate on the wall next to the waiting room. It is in Cyrillic so I cannot say what occasion it marks, but the year whatever happened when it happened was 1923.

A pair of benches sits on either side of the ticket office entrance, occupied by half a dozen passengers. Like those in traffic queues, they seem quite content to sit and wait. A man in an 80s-style suit has a similarly Yuppie-era metal briefcase on his lap, but I am disappointed that he is not consulting a Filofax. Beside him is an elderly couple who look much-married and yet still holding hands. Next to them is a solid, plainly dressed and somehow country-looking woman. She has her arms clasped around a basket on her lap and is looking with slight irritation at a younger woman who is waving her free hand about and speaking dramatically into the mobile phone clamped to her ear. I look at her and suddenly realise it is the first mobile phone I have seen in use in Berkovitsa.

This is literally the end of the line, and, as my guide book says, it connects Berkovitsa with the rest of the world. The service runs regularly each day to Montana, from where trains can be taken to other places, including Sofia.

This and most of the other stations, services and rolling stock in the country are owned and run by the Bulgarian State Railway. As with Britain in the 1960s, the railway system is coming under severe pressure from other forms of transport, but as yet there has been no Slavic Dr Beeching arriving with his axe. There is a competing bus service to Montana, and the journey for goods would obviously be quicker by road. As the staff outnumber the passengers this morning, I assume this outpost of the system is running at a loss. The station looks as if it is a hangover from the past, and is the sort of place that is only mourned when it is gone forever.

~

Probably with good reason, Bulgarians seem generally frugal with electricity. Lights are certainly not much in evidence inside the ticket office, which is a large, high-ceilinged room, its panelled walls covered in posters and timetables.

Behind a narrow desk sits a very wide man who seems to be melting and overflowing from his chair. Like his fellow employees, he is wearing a high-visibility jacket. This is helpful as it stops me bumping into his workmates on my way to the desk.

The man is looking down at some sheets of paper, but I can tell from the way he looks up and smiles immediately I arrive that he is going to be helpful. All regular train travellers will know that railway workers are divided into two main types. One is happy or even keen to cope with questions and pass on helpful information. The other regards any approach as a potential assault or at least an intrusion on his or her personal space. He or she will also believe that all information about the station and train services are private, and not to be passed on to members of the public unless in very exceptional circumstances.

This man comes into category one, and actually looks pleased to join in the mime game. As the train goes nowhere else but Montana, I don't have much of a problem explaining my destination; he shakes his head to show he understands, then levers himself up and leads me to a wall to point out the next departure time.

Back at the desk, he picks up what looks like a block of raffle tickets, then calls out in polite and surprisingly high-pitched tones. The handle turns on a door in the partition behind the man at the desk, and I notice that the two loungers stand a little straighter.

The door opens and a tall and authoritative figure appears. He is wearing a dark-coloured uniform of jacket and trousers in some sort of heavy material. Although inside, he also wears a peaked hat with a red top which is a more restrained version of the Soviet officer's headwear that Kratzi likes to wear.

The man, who I take to be the station master, nods gravely, and I am now schooled well enough in nodding procedure in Bulgaria to know it is a positive rather than a negative gesture. As well as signalling 'yes' or 'no' depending on the user, it may also be used in the standard western European mode as a greeting. This one is a version of the regal acknowledgement Mother Russia bestows when we meet on the road to the village shop. The tall man now exchanges a few words with my large friend, who tears off one of the tickets and passes it to his superior. The uniformed man examines it, then takes a pen from inside his jacket, signs the slip and returns it to the wide man. I nod my thanks and hold out some money. The station master flinches and steps back a little, and the seated man smiles reassuringly, reaches out and takes the 20 leva note. He gives me almost the same amount back in change, and we both shake our heads and smile. Business concluded, the station master gives a final nod and retreats into his office. I walk back out into the sunlight, feeling somehow special. One could hardly expect Virgin Rail to deal with its high volume of customers on such a personal level, but it would certainly help with their image.

~

The little man is frantically turning the big wheel on the other side of the tracks, so I know our train must be on its way.

As I and my fellow-travellers stand and gather their belongings, the station master walks with dignified pace onto the platform. I note he has buttoned his jacket, straightened his hat, and has what looks like an army officer's swagger stick tucked under his right arm. He is holding on to its end as he marches to the edge of the platform, and, once there, he stands ramrod-straight as the train rumbles to a stop. At first I think there has been a mistake as it is on a set of rails some distance from the platform. Then I see the other passengers walking down an incline and crossing the tracks between us and the new arrival. I follow, confident that there is no danger as the power is coming from overhead rather than the line. We arrive at a narrow, raised strip of concrete running alongside the train, and I reach up to one of the handles. A hand touches my arm and I see it is the lady with the basket. She smiles and inclines her head in what I know is a politely negative nod.

Suddenly, a short man in an even shorter uniform bursts from the ticket office and sprints past the station master and across the gap to join us. I see he is wearing a money pouch and what looks like a ticket punch, worn in a cross-bandolier style, like an old-fashioned bus conductor. A sliding door opens, and he looks back at the station master to get assent before shepherding us on board. It is quite a climb, so I get on first and give the countrified lady a hand up. She smiles her thanks and I offer my hand to the phone woman, but she is still talking and hauls herself up and past me into the carriage. Within her little world, I obviously do not exist.

When we are all aboard, the door closes and I look out of a grimy window to see if the station master will blow a whistle or wave his flag. In fact, he turns on his heel and marches smartly back into the station.

The train pulls gently away and we spread ourselves around. It is open-plan and rather like a London Underground carriage, except there are no advertisements and only a fraction of the travellers. Clean and un-vandalised blue fabric seats line either side of a central aisle, and above them, commodious netting-style racks run the length of the carriage. Just this single carriage could hold forty customers and the elbow room would seem like paradise to any Tube commuter, but can't bode well for the future of this branch line. I do a tally of my fellow passengers and work out that, if they have paid the same fare as me, the Bulgarian State Railway has grossed the equivalent of eight pounds for taking us on the fifteen-mile, one hour journey.

~

The man with the briefcase and the husband-and-wife couple have moved further up the carriage, while I have taken a seat on the other side of the aisle from the lady with the basket. The woman with the phone could have had her own carriage in which to have her conversation, but predictably chose to throw herself dramatically on to a seat where she will have us as an audience.

It is a curious fact that, in spite of its relatively tiny population, Bulgaria is the second biggest consumer of Turkish soap operas in terms of viewing figures per head.

There are 27 soaps currently on offer, and I bet this lady watches them all.

Free from the terrors of driving, I sit back and look out at the passing landscape. We are on a plain, and it is not impressive. The track mostly follows the road and the view is limited to the flat, shrub-covered terrain, power pylons, dilapidated buildings and passing traffic. The cars and lorries and assorted vehicles are doing at least four times the speed of the train, but we get our revenge when the barriers come down as we approach a crossing. They are surprisingly frequent, and I enjoy smiling at the same truck driver each time we limp past.

Back in the carriage, the woman with the phone has apparently not paused for breath. Of course I cannot understand what she is saying, but unless there is nobody on the other end and she is talking just for effect, it is clearly an emotionally-charged conversation. She occasionally sneaks a look to see if we are watching, then ups the tempo and throws her arms around ever more extravagantly.

Opposite, the lady with the basket has tuned the phone woman out and is looking out of the window with an almost serene expression. She has what we westerners think of as a wonderfully typical Slavic face, and I wonder just what her deep-set, lustrous eyes have observed over the past sixty years or so. Much more than the phone woman, without a doubt. I have yet to figure out whether character is formed by experience or merely handed out like a deck of cards; whatever it is, I reckon these two women are at opposite ends of the emotionally mature spectrum.

~

We are nearing civilisation, and the outskirts of Montana remind me of the view of Sofia from the airplane window, but not on such a grand scale.

There are the now-familiar unfinished building projects, the rows of frowzy apartment blocks, and the wasteland areas containing wrecked cars and piles of rubbish. I am sure Montana will be much more appealing when we reach the centre, but the vista underlines the fact that this is the chief town of the poorest part of a very poor country. Curiously, the train is picking up speed rather than slowing down as we near journey's end, and I wonder if this is to hurry us through the unsavoury sights of the suburbs.

~

The station master at Montana is much shorter than her counterpart at Berkovitsa, in spite of a pair of slinky high heels. She also takes a more relaxed approach to meeting a train, and manages to make the event look almost erotic as she sashays across the platform and waves her baton around.

I am first off, and offer a hand to the lady with the basket. She smiles and holds my look for a few seconds before walking off towards the exit. Though we are divided by a different language and culture, I think we both know we share the same philosophy, at least with regard to drama queens performing on mobile telephones. It is sad that I can never know her story, how the world has treated her and what she thinks of it. As I watch her walk away, the woman with the phone pushes past, still talking and never listening.

I follow her out of the station, but am drawn to a huge greenhouse with very dirty windows. I spit on a pane and rub off a layer of grime, and see the building houses a perfectly restored steam locomotive. I am no expert, but it looks of the same vintage as me. It is almost garishly painted and has white wall wheels, and is coupled to a flatbed bogie which carries a small field gun. It is a sober olive colour, but the wheel rims have been painted white to colour-coordinate with the locomotive. There is no plaque that I can see and I would not be able to read it anyway, so will never know what part the train and gun played in the often turbulent past of Montana.

Coming out of the station, I am reminded of the centre of Sofia. Not so much by the communist-era statues and architecture, but by the traffic density and lunatic driving. After my time in Krasiva and Berkovitsa, the sound and fury are magnified and it is a challenge just to cross the dual carriageway. There is also a smell which is familiar but unwelcome, and one I have been free of for several weeks. It is a melange of sooty smelling and acrid fumes, and I realise it is the smell which dominates wherever motor vehicles swarm in great numbers.

~

New York may be so good they named it twice, but Montana can beat that hands down. The number of identities the town has gone through makes it seem like a dodgy company which keeps changing its name to avoid paying its debts.

The Roman city of Montanensium was founded in AD160 and there are the remains of a fort to prove it. When the Slavs moved in several centuries later, the settlement was christened Kutofça or Kutlovitsa. In 1890 it was re-named Ferdinand in honour of the then prince of Bulgaria. Then 1945 brought another bonus for map and sign makers when the snappy title of Mihaylovgrad was devised to honour a party activist who died in the September Rising of 1923. Finally and after a presidential decree in 1993, the name game went full circle and the Latin name for 'mountain' was restored. Nowadays about 40,000 people call Montana home, which is down from its peak in the 1990s. But the decrease in residents has been more than matched by the increase in traffic. This is because the town is what my guide book calls a major transport hub. The guide also finds Montana 'unappealing', and grudgingly recommends a hotel for travellers who, as it says, get stuck there for the night.

~

Whatever is said about communism being bad for art and design, the practitioners certainly knew how to do big statues and squares.

As with Berkovitsa, major cement suppliers and concrete mixer makers would have made a fortune when Montana was rebuilt along communist lines. In spite of that, the centre has a quite sophisticated air.

The square is on different levels, has some attractive green areas and is liberally sprinkled with fountains. As in Berkovitsa, the Montanans clearly have a thriving café society, and the centre is awash with bars and restaurants and kiosks, their entrances guarded by regiments of tables, chairs and gay umbrellas. The bars are outnumbered by the usual stern and spookily lifelike stone men, but there are plenty of real people. A hunch of old men play what looks like the Bulgarian version of French boules, and young mums push prams, stop to greet friends or sit by the fountains and shout at their toddlers. On a sandy patch, children perform stunts on mountain bikes. These young people are the town, region and country's future, so I hope they choose to stay and help make it a better place in which to live.

I stop at a hybrid between a kiosk and a bar, where a group of teenage girls are practicing their English. They find nothing odd about a strange old man asking them where he can buy a pair of baggy shorts, and we are soon chatting about their lives in Montana and their plans for the future. Two out of the half dozen want to leave the country when they finish their education, and both want to live and work in England (it is always 'England' that they stipulate as their dream destination, and never the UK or Britain). The others have not made their minds up, but say they like the idea of living in England. They are quite candid that what attracts them is what they hear about amazingly high wages and an exciting social life.

They don't seem worried when I explain that my iced coffee would cost ten times as much in a trendy London café-bar.

~

Perhaps unsurprisingly, second-hand clothes shops seem popular in this part of Bulgaria. They are like our charity shops, but the charity begins at home as they are commercial enterprises. I know of three in Berkovitsa and have already seen many more in Montana. They all seem well-patronised, and the one I am in has so much stock there is little room for customers. Dresses and coats and jumpers and suits hang from the ceiling as well as the closely-spaced rows of rails, and the window is so filled with piles of shoes and boots and trainers that the light hardly penetrates. There are also large cardboard rummage boxes brimful with garments the owners didn't feel worth putting on show. A dozen customers are picking their way round the shop floor, and two women are on duty at the counter. One is taking the money and handing over the goods, but not until the other woman has weighed them and announced the price. I have never seen clothing sold by weight before, but as I am looking for a roomy pair of durable shorts for a hiking expedition, I suspect I will be paying top whack.

After working my way along the rails and through the boxes, I see a very large pair of khaki cargo pants hanging from the ceiling in the far corner. They have several patch pockets on the legs and lots of impressively accommodating belt loops to hang knives and rope ladders from, so look just the job. They are not shorts, but I have a pair of scissors at the guest house. Unfortunately, another customer has also spotted them. He is wider and taller than me, and beats me to the target by simply parting the rails with two massive hands and forging straight ahead to the target. My competitive spirit kindled, I lunge forward and grab the leg he is not holding. We stand facing each other until he inflates his massive chest, glares down at me and takes a double-handed grip on his leg. Not wanting to cause an international incident, I acknowledge defeat and watch him carry his prize triumphantly to the counter.

Ten minutes later I leave with my find. They are not exactly what I was looking for as they are a pair of very narrow-legged pantaloons of some sort of shiny material. They are pocketless, have vertical stripes of blue and white, and look exactly like the legwear favoured by Rod Stewart in his *Maggie May* days. They are not a patch on the trousers I missed out on, but I comfort myself with the thought that, because of the charge-by-weight system they cost a fraction of the price.

~

Another contrast with the UK.

In Britain, some taxi drivers seem to take a pride in driving faster and much more aggressively, arrogantly and stupidly than civilians. Here, the opposite seems to apply. Everyday Bulgarian drivers would make British cabbies appear cautious and considerate, but taxi drivers here make little old ladies behind the wheel in Britain look like road hogs.

After wondering around the market and resisting the allure of a World War II despatch rider's motorcycle, a full-size Bowie knife and a very lifelike AK47 assault rifle, I decided to take a taxi back to Berkovitsa. Asking directions in mime-speak, I passed a line of cars I thought were waiting to be towed away to the nearest breaker's yard before realising it was a taxi rank. Entered into a Most Unkempt Motor contest, they would all have beaten Richard's Lada hands down.

It is generally accepted that a two-price system is not uncommon in Bulgaria, and foreigners can be asked to pay more for some goods and services. The internet is full of horror stories about massive overcharging for taxi rides, with some victims being asked for even more than the fare would be in the UK.

Accordingly I hid round the nearest corner with my Canny Traveller's phrase book and practiced 'How much to Berkovitsa and don't try it on, mate' before approaching the car at the head of the queue. The small man behind the wheel clearly did not speak his own language well, so it was mime time. He let me go on for a while before asking my destination in near-perfect English, marred only by his dropping of his aitches and use of cockney rhyming slang.

~

My father used to say that timing was as important as luck as we travel through life, and I think he was right. Five minutes sooner or later and I would never have met Bogdan.

The name means 'a gift from the gods' and the ancient Thracian deities have certainly done me proud. Bogdan worked in the meat market in London's Smithfield for a decade, so swears a lot and speaks colloquial English with a slight cockney accent. As I searched for my seat under a pile of chocolate bar wrappers, banana skins, orange peel, newspapers, crumpled - up betting slips and empty cigarette packets and soft drink cans and the odd dead cat, he explained that all taxis are required by municipal law to display their charges on the windscreen and on the dashboard directly in front of the passenger seat. He did not say, but I am guessing there is no municipal minimum requirement for health and hygiene standards in registered taxis.

~

With a surface area of twenty-four hectares, the reservoir at Montana is one of the biggest in Europe. It collects the water from three rivers and stands on the very edge of and sixty feet above the suburbs of Montana. It is interesting to think what would happen if the dam was breached. Three villages lie beneath the surface of the artificial lake, and were sacrificed to set up an ambitious irrigation system. It never happened, and now the lake services two hydro-electric power stations.

In 1999 the reservoir was stocked for commercial fishing, and holds dozens of species. The locals say it is not safe to swim in the lake because shark-sized and potentially man-eating catfish lurk in the depths. This may also be the reason the huge expanse of water seems to have no boats on it. It may also be the reason for the popularity of the swimming facilities at the leisure complex overlooking the lake. We had a beer there and watched as children and adults frolicked in the two pools, while waiters scurried about serving food at silly prices to foreign visitors.

~

In 160 AD, a Roman military camp was established on an ancient Thracian settlement where Montana now stands. It developed into one of the most important Roman towns in the province, but the only evidence it was ever there is the remains of a hill fort overlooking the reservoir. It is the third Roman hill fort I have visited, and as disappointing as the other two. Like an ancient version of the unfinished buildings on the outskirts of the town, it is no more than a series of large blocks of stone, which have been cemented together in recent times. The result looks like a waist-high maze or the groundworks and foundations laid before the building work started. I don't see how the archaeologists knew where the blocks should be put and stuck together, so ask Bogdan. He shrugs and says some disappointed metal-detecting looters believe there never was a fort there, and the tourist board made it up to attract visitors and give the town extra status.

~

The fare to Berkovitsa including the detours was less than a fiver. We shook hands beside the Lada and I saw Bogdan cast an admiring glance at the detritus inside. He refused the offer of a beer at the pub across the road because he said, like me, he would rather have no beer than just one; and had to drive back to Montana. The police here can be hot on drink-driving, he said, though it is generally accepted that drunk drivers usually show more road sense than sober ones.

We hugged, then parted like old friends after making a date for my return visit to Montana. He said he would take a day off and show me the interesting parts of the town that visitors never get to see.

I shall look forward to that. All my guide books agree that Montana is worth no more than a fleeting visit, but I think it is the people who make any place interesting, and much more so than scrubbed-up ancient buildings and haughty museums.

~

My way home is marked by a runway of glowing green dots. A child of the town might think someone had planted a series of light-emitting diodes in the verge. I know them as companions on many an after-dark summer walk in the countryside. To bug hunters they are *Lampyris noctiluca*, and to us they are glow worms. In fact they are not worms, but beetles, and only the females emit that little green light. The lights glow to attract flying males, and are turned off when mating has taken place. The females die shortly after laying their eggs, and the eternal cycle begins again. There are fan clubs for glow worms across Europe and as far afield as Nepal.

I am walking my rather unsteady way home after dinner at Sally and Richard's, then a nightcap with the only other British expatriate in the village. Or in fact, the only other person in the village who was not born here or in Berkovitsa.

The meal was to mark the return of Roger Smith from the UK to take up permanent residence in Krasiva, and the return from elsewhere in Bulgaria of the Moore's friend, translator, clerk of the works and general Mr Fixit.

Ivailo Lazarov is a man of average height and appears to be in early middle age. I don't think his age is a secret, but I did not ask as he strikes me as someone who is not keen on releasing anything he would see as personal information.

My first impression was that everything about him was neat and clean and - either because or in spite of that - somehow menacing. The neatness extended from his short, carefully cut hair to his casual but smart clothing and even his fingernails. I imagine that this physical orderliness extends to his mind. He drank and spoke little during the meal, but saw all. Perhaps he seemed so guarded because we had not met before and he is obviously a very private man. I think it will take time to get to know him, and then only if he is willing.

Sitting opposite the Moore's action man, Roger Smith seems as open as Ivo Lazarov is self-contained. He is an elderly, short, rotund man with a large head and features and a taste for very accommodating loud shorts and shirts. He has a ready smile, likes to talk and has a real story to tell. In fact, he has many stories about his life and adventures which make for interesting listening.

For the last six years he has been converting three shaky walls into a home with the best view in the village, and plans to spend the rest of his days in it.

Unlike most people who buy a home or move to live in a foreign country, Roger is not a first-timer. He lived for a decade in the south of France, so knows what it is like to be a permanent newcomer.

I have met and interviewed many British expatriates, and know that people move to a new country and a new life for a number of reasons. Sadly, they are usually the wrong reasons. Some go to where the weather, price of property and the cost of living are cheaper, which is not a good basis for changing your life and leaving friends and family behind. Others move abroad to re-invigorate or save a failing relationship, and the opposite invariably happens. I have found that the ones who seem to do best are those with an open and curious mind and a resilience to the occasional culture clash and setback. A good sense of humour is also a must. For the solitary expat, the additional calls on character and attitude are considerable. The individual stranger in a strange land must be happy or at least content to be alone. Roger Smith is unusual in that he is clearly fond of company when there is some, but from what he said seems to manage perfectly well without it.

~

I have reached the guest house, and hear a movement in Madame-next-door's yard. Muttley is lying on his belly, regarding me with a reflective expression and obviously resting up before the exertions of his barking duties during the night. Ironically, there was not as much as a growl or grumble from any of the village dogs I passed on my way home. They have come to recognise my smell and can't be bothered to waste their breaths before its time to limber up for the night chorus. I think of trying to curry favour with him, but decide it might be taken as a sign of weakness.

Instead I give him a neutral nod, then stand on the landing and take a long breath of the sweet, cool air. For the moment all is still, and, across the valley, Kom sleeps beneath a bedspread of stars.

I let myself in, and as I reach for the light switch I see a wonderful sight. Tiny pinpoints of light are dancing in the passageway, ducking and bobbing and weaving. I shake my head to clear the effects of the *Rakia* nightcap, then realise what I am seeing. After the glow worms have seen me safely home, a trio of fireflies are lighting my way to bed.

A big breakfast favourite with children in Bulgaria and throughout the region is another way of using up unwanted or stale bread. In Greece it is called *maza*, in Turkey *tirit,* and in Spain *migas*. There is even a Tex-Mex version in the United States which uses tortillas and comes with onion and bell peppers. We would call it bread and milk, but to Bulgarian mums and their families it is:

Попара
Popara
(cheesy bread and milk)

Ingredients

Some stale bread with crusts removed
Some milk
Some feta-style cheese
A knob of butter

Method

1. Boil some milk
2. Tear the bread into pieces and mix in a bowl with the cheese
3. Pour the boiling milk over the bread and cheese
4. Cover and leave for five minutes before adding the butter and serving

As evidenced by their national dish and like other Slavic races, Bulgarians are big on salads. This traditional favourite has been borrowed and adapted from their Soviet near-neighbours:

руска салата
ruska salata
(Russian salad)

Ingredients

500g diced potatoes
200g chopped carrots
200g peas
200g chopped spring onions
300g chopped ham
100g corn niblets*

Method

1. Boil the potatoes, carrots and peas
2. When cooled, mix all ingredients together
3. Keep in fridge until just before serving

*A common sight at any market is a stall selling cups of corn niblets. Corn is also a fashionable item to feature in the 'nouvelle cuisine' approach to Bulgarian dishes.

Carp has always been a favourite dish in eastern Europe. It used to be in Britain, when every monastery had its carp pond. Until recently, members of the *Cyprinidae* family would have felt safe swimming in UK waters. They are a very hard fish to catch, and after spending hours hooking one, the tradition is to return it for the next angler to take on. But the British carp has not been so safe since the influx of eastern Europeans. A lot of stories about migrants and their funny ways are tosh, but it is true that the Environmental Agency has had to set up patrols to stop the illegal harvesting of carp with nets.

Having caught their carp, Bulgarians like to cook and eat it in a variety of ways. This one is a traditional favourite:

пълнени шаран с орехи

ulneni sharan s orekhi

(stuffed carp with walnuts)

Ingredients

A whole carp (about 2 kilo)
100g of rice
50g of butter
One grated carrot
Two chopped onions
200g sliced mushrooms
A pinch of thyme
A pinch of savory
A bunch of parsley, chopped
Two large tomatoes, diced
A cup of walnuts
Some slices of lemon and tomato
Juice of a lemon
Salt and black pepper
Some mixed spice

Method

1. Clean the fish by taking out the guts and cutting off the fins
2. Rinse thoroughly under cold water, dry and season inside and out
3. Drizzle with lemon juice and allow to marinade for half an hour
4. Cook the rice
5. In a large pan, sauté the onions, walnuts, carrot and mushrooms
6. Season
7. When finished cooking, add the rice, thyme, savory, chopped parsley, black pepper and chopped tomatoes
8. Mix well and add some salt to taste
9. Stuff the carp
10. Close the wound and secure with toothpicks
11. Rub the skin of the fish with the mixed spices
12. Put the fish into an oven bag, laying the surplus stuffing and sliced tomatoes and lemon around it
13. Bake at 180°C for the best part of an hour
14. Open the bag at the top and let the carp brown for half an hour

Wherever apples grow you will find apple cake and pie is a speciality, and Bulgaria is no exception. Sometimes walnuts are added, but this is the basic recipe:

Български ябълков сладкиш
Bulgarski yabulkov sladkish
(Bulgarian apple cake)

Ingredients

A large eating apple (soft and yellow is recommended)
Two tablespoons of butter
Two eggs
Half a cup of flour
Half a cup of sugar
Two tablespoonfuls of milk powder
A splash of milk
A tablespoon of baking powder
A few drops of vanilla essence
A pinch of cinnamon
Some whipped cream
A baking dish

Method

1. Peel and then cut the apple into very thin slices
2. Put the butter in the dish and put in a medium-hot oven, taking it out when the butter has melted
3. In a mixing bowl, beat the eggs with the sugar. Add the melted butter, the flour, the powdered milk, the wet milk, the baking powder, the vanilla and cinnamon and beat gently until well mixed.
4. Make a layer or more of the apple slices in the dish and pour the cake mixture over
5. Bake until golden. Then let it cool before you invert the cake on a plate and cover the top with whipped cream

Полевите изследвания
Field studies

House flies: 132
Horse flies: 49
Wasps: 6
Other: 3

The fact that there are more donkeys than cars in Krasiva is probably why so many fly families like to come here on holiday.

The sticky paper hanging in the hall, kitchen, bedroom and sitting room may have been hard to find and buy, but is proving a deadly weapon in the battle against flying pests. Fly swatters work and are effective but are hard work and can be dangerous to ornaments and people. Electronic insect repellent or killing devices are not available in Berkovitsa, but, if you can unroll and pin them up without becoming a victim to the glutinous coating, flypapers work a treat. Part of the reason for their success must be because of the sheer numbers of house invaders, but, as with cheese-baited mousetraps, sometimes the old ways are the best.

Today could be the cause for a double celebration, as along with the fly invasion I think I may have solved the dog problem.

Muttley started up within an hour of my falling asleep at midnight, and was immediately joined by the other members of his quartet.

To my shame, still muzzy from the beer and wine and *Rakia* and in a desperate, unthinking rage, I stumbled out of bed, flung open the door on to the balcony and bellowed:

'SHUT THE FUCKING FUCK UP!'

My imprecation rolled around the valley and, quite eerily, the baying and barking stopped immediately. Most significantly, it did not restart all night.

I woke refreshed but feeling bad about bellowing profanities from a balcony in the middle of the night in a neighbourhood where I am a guest. There is some consolation in that nobody in earshot would understand what I shouted, and Ivalin says Madame next-door is very hard of hearing. Most importantly, my despairing over-reaction worked. The trick now will be to maintain the ceasefire.

~

I am on my morning walk around the village, and so far there have been no negative reactions to my attack of Tourette's Syndrome. Muttley was as usual lying doggo in the road outside his front gate, and actually gave a feeble and what I took to be placatory wag of his tail as I approached. He wagged it even harder when I threw him a chocolate bar. Perhaps I should not have shown weakness with a pay-off gift, but I would rather keep him in Twix bars than have to bellow from the balcony every night.

Another busy morning in Krasiva as Old Ivan and Angel clopped by on their carts, followed by Mr Rotavator.

Angel is a local bigwig as he is the owner of the only cow in the village. There is a small herd which grazes in the valley, but it is owned by a syndicate from Berkovitsa. In England people have weekend cottages; here they have weekend cows and vineyards.

Angel is also distinguished by having a satellite dish outside his house. He is a genuine character, and so is his long-eared donkey. When we first met, he said through Sally Moore that his Donkey Pancho is named after the servant in the book about the Spanish gentleman who tilted at windmills.

Following the cart and the Rotavator, the village bus tootled past, then Mr Big ripped by in the middle of the lane. He gave a blast on the horn and waved almost amicably, so perhaps my mystery guardian angel has had a word with him.

In the square I find much excitement. A small crowd has gathered around an enormous and ancient flatbed lorry. It wears huge tractor wheels and the remains of a khaki paint job, and the outline of a communist star shows faintly on each door. It is probably post-War in vintage, but that could be post the Great War.

Announcing its arrival with a fit of coughing and snorting and belching, a smaller version of the lorry struggles in to the square from the track leading down through the valley and into the forest. It is laden with logs, each one at least twenty feet in length. They still bear stubs of branches, and looks as if they have been loaded hastily before proper trimming and preparation.

As an excited Kratzi directs with windmill arms, the lorry pulls up alongside its big brother and disgorges three men. They wear no uniforms, and scramble up on to the back and begin to manhandle the logs across and on to the bigger truck. Elsewhere in Europe, health and safety rules would apply, and there would probably be a hydraulic grab to pick the logs up and swing them across the divide. Here, it is all handraulic, and the three men make shifting the several tons of tree trunks look easy.

Although we are in the midst of a heat wave, in a few months the snow will lay deep across the valley and the temperatures will drop to ten degrees below zero. Most households will get through ten cubic metres of wood for heating before spring arrives, and, though the hills and vales of this country are densely forested, firewood from official sources is not cheap. That is why there is a flourishing trade in unofficial fuel. Pine is much inferior to oak and burns quicker and colder, but is much cheaper bought off the back of an unmarked lorry.

The whole operation is completed in not much more than half an hour. As the two trucks and the men were in mufti, it is unlikely they are from the Forestry authority or a company working on their behalf. Even if the trees have been harvested illegally, I have to admire the way the men showed that there is still a place for manly skills and strength in modern times.

~

Thirteen percent of the population of the Montana region is made up of Roma gypsies, which is the highest density in Bulgaria. As well as being the largest ethnic minority, they have the highest birth rate. In fact, they have the highest birth rate in Europe. In surveys, up to eighty percent of Bulgarians admit to negative feelings towards the *Tsigani*. Five times as many Roma live under the poverty line. They make up seventy percent of the prison population, while 0.3 percent go to university. Although happy to employ Roma as cheap labour, some Bulgarians will not allow them to enter the house.

I have been looking at the history of the race and its

trials as Ivalin Dimitrov employs only Roma women and has invited me to join them for a day in his raspberry fields.

My workmates are gathered around a table in the yard, drinking what looks like treacly black coffee from tiny cups. They are waiting as Ivalin works on the latest problem with his van. He assures me it is nothing major, just a new wheel to replace the one he lost on the way back to the factory yesterday.

I am introduced to Tina, Derina, Rose and Donka, and take the opportunity to try out my entire Romany vocabulary. From their blank expressions, Hampshire and Bulgarian gypsies do not speak the same language. The women look at me with open curiosity, but no hostility or concern. Ivalin tells me he has already told them I am mad, which he says will explain everything and like in many ancient cultures people with mental health problems are treated with respect and concern.

The four women range from young to late middle-age, and there is no mistaking their ethnicity. They have a natural deep colouring many western women strive to attain at great cost, dark eyes, raven-black hair and strong features.

After the introductions, I put a box of doughnuts on the table. I am not patronising them, as I would have done the same had they been factory workers in England I was to spend the day with. They look at each other and then at Ivalin and I can see they are not asking permission, but if the doughnuts are for them. He nods and one of the women opens the box and hands them round. The younger one says something and the rest of the women laugh. Their teeth are very white against their richly tanned skin, but only the youngest has a full smile.

Ten minutes later and I have pretended to enjoy the coffee and what are, Ivalin tells me, the very ribald jokes. The van is ready, and we are invited to board. I move to join the ladies in the back, but Ivalin insists I take the front passenger seat. There are no safety belts, and we are off through the gates as soon as the doors are slammed.

~

I thought Ivalin was reckless when speeding through the village, but off-road he drives faster and, if it were possible, even more insanely. The potholed tarmac has been replaced by a sun-baked dirt track, riven with deep tractor ruts. It also winds sharply, and slopes alarming steeply downhill into the valley. Before we left, Ivalin told me that the fields are in secret locations and I jokingly asked if I would need to wear a blindfold. Now I wish I had.

As we veer crazily close to the edge of the track and the sheer drop alongside, it seems to me that Ivalin is actually flirting with the deepest of the ruts and deliberately getting perilously close to the drop. I don't think he is doing it to impress the Roma women or frighten me, but is driving like a madman for the same reason some people jump out of airplanes or go bungee jumping. It will be the same reason he climbs mountains in the worst conditions. He likes the charge of adrenalin and is a natural risk-taker. Setting up a business in a remote area of the poorest part of Bulgaria, I suppose he would have to be.

~

Down and down the spiral track we rock and roll and shake and shudder. I have ridden trail bikes over the roughest terrain and been a passenger in many an off-road vehicle, but they were nothing compared to this. With no seat belts or crash helmets and protective clothing, we are bouncing around in an ancient Transit with lots of sharp and knobbly projections.

I snatch a look over my shoulder, and see that the Roma

girls are literally unmoved by what for them will be a familiar experience. All four have wedged themselves onto one of the two bench seats, and are using long-handled hoes and spades as barge poles to fend off danger and keep themselves in place.

Suddenly, we lurch off the track and I breathe a sigh of relief as we are faced with a small, swiftly flowing river and beyond it, an impenetrable wall of trees. We have obviously arrived and are at journey's end. As I reach for the door handle, Ivalin stays my hand and steps on the accelerator. We lurch across a stretch of grass, bounce and splash across the stream and squeeze through a gap between two giant pine trees, and I realise why there are no wing mirrors on the Transit.

There is some consolation that the way through the forest is on the level and there are trees rather than sheer drops on each side. The relief is such that I begin to unclench my buttocks and take notice of our new surroundings.

We are heading for the heart of the huge, densely treed forest I look at from the balcony of the guest house every day. The mix of pine and deciduous trees compete for space and light, and so have grown tall and spindly. Completely unmanaged, all is as nature intended and it is nature's law of the survival of the strongest. Some giant firs have reached the end of their lives, toppled over and lie recumbent. The trees are so tightly packed that some have not made it to the ground and lay propped up against a neighbour.

So dense is the forest that it is in a perennial twilight, broken by bright shafts in which motes of dust, scraps of leaves dance and insects cavort.

Then there is light at the end of the tunnel and we break through into a clearing. The sun is once again the master of the sky, and the light sparkles off a stream which may be the one we forded earlier. Criss-crossing the clearing are rows of man-high raspberry bushes, and alongside is what looks like a small cemetery filled with crudely-made crosses.

We disembark, and three of the Roma women make straight for the raspberry plantation. The youngest takes a selection of gardening tools and heads for a large allotment alongside the stream.

Ivalin takes me on a tour of his secret gardens, and explains that the wooden crosses are supports for young grapevines. Guarding the allotment is a hedge of tall barley, grown for Ivalin's donkey but ravaged by the wild boar that come to the river to drink.

Lined with orderly ranks of runner and broad beans, beetroot, onion sets and lettuces, the allotment looks strangely out of place in the heart of a deep, dark Bulgarian forest, and Ivalin explains he has grown what he calls the English vegetables from seed for Roger. I will see from the size and shape and colour of the tomatoes that they are Bulgarian.

After the tour of his secret acres, Ivalin says it is time for me to earn my wages. I am given a stack of plastic trays and shown how to pick the fruit without damaging it. He explains that, like the vegetables, the raspberries are English, so I should be naturally suited to harvest them. He hastens to add that they are not as sweet as Bulgarian varieties, but suit being used for confectionery rather than eating.

After an hour, I have eaten or spoiled more than I have picked. My back aches and my face and fingers are stained a guilty red. Ivalin shakes his head and tips my pathetic offering into a single tray in the stack already assembled by the Roma ladies. I have taken part in many a *vendange* grape harvest in France, and the pickers here have that same practiced economy and ease of movement. They move almost balletically along the rows, bending and stretching and gathering the fruit with a grace which confirms there can be dignity in labour.

~

Ivalin's mood has changed. We are further along the bank and at a sharp bend in the stream. The water races through the oxbow, but is no more than a few inches deep. Although easily fordable, there is a small stone bridge across it. The structure is almost ornamental, it is no more than a yard wide and was obviously a labour of creation rather than a practical solution. There is a brass plaque set into the low parapet and on it some words and a date.

I can see that Ivalin is deeply moved, and I wait until he is ready to explain.

He built the bridge, he says, in memory of his mother, and so that no-one else would suffer her fate.

After a long pause, he goes on to explain that this part of the forest and river had belonged to the family since his grandparents had bought it, and it had remained in family hands during the communist regime simply because they did not know about it. Every day, his mother would come along this trail with her donkey. At the start of the new Millennium and in her 72nd year, she was crossing the stream at this point when she must have stumbled and fallen and been unable to get up. She drowned in no more than two inches of water, and was found after the donkey returned to the family home alone.

We stand and look at the bridge for a moment and I try and imagine what it must have been for a young Ivalin to find his mother lying face down in the water. Then he gives a big, shuddering sigh, softly says something, turns away and leads me back to his secret gardens.

~

I am in the van with Ivalin, and the going is even tougher. We left the Roma girls at the raspberry plantation, and he is taking me to see his strawberry fields the hard way.

After retracing our path through the forest and over the stream, we left the track and headed uphill across open ground. It was a mercifully short journey before we arrived on a plateau half way up the valley slopes. In the distance on one side were the tawny roofs of the village, and on the other the Planina range continues its march eastwards. It is an almost achingly beautiful location for a small agricultural enterprise.

By a battered shed, a gate leads to the start of row after row of strawberry plants descending a gentle slope. We walked along a central aisle, and I lost count after four hundred plants. Like a proud father, Ivalin said that the last of the fruit went to the confectionery factory in Sofia a month ago, but the plants have begun to flower again. This was more than unusual at this height.

It was a particularly dry and hot summer, but he had kept the plants well watered. He showed me the lines of pierced plastic piping along each row, and when I asked where the water came from, he pointed towards the forest. Damming the stream had created a small lake, from where the water is pumped up. When I asked if he built the dam, he said no, but that the villagers are glad to have such a convenient fishing lake. I said I would like to have a dip there now, but he replied that it is full of catfish which make the man-eaters at Montana look like tiddlers.

Before we left, I suggested he could set up and advertise a pick-your-own system. When I explained how PYO works in the UK he laughed dryly and said it would certainly not work here. Being Bulgarian, the visitors would pick and eat all the fruit and expect not to have to pay for it.

He looked at his watch and said it was time to return to the raspberry fields, but he has something special to show me first. There is a spring nearby dedicated to a Roman goddess and not even the country's leading archaeologists know of it. Before I asked why it was unknown, I knew what he was going to say. The source is in a place which is practically inaccessible to any vehicles.

~

A half hour on, and we are stuck fast.

We had been bumping downhill at the usual mad rate when we hit a morass. Even in this arid summer, the track ahead was under water. Ivalin pulled up and said something must have blocked the source and diverted the water away from its course to the stream. As the water lapped around the front wheels, even he had to admit defeat. It would have been simpler to back up, but Ivalin could not resist the challenge of doing a three-point-turn on a waterlogged track barely wider than the van. One side was edged with a massive bramble bush, the other dropped away sharply downhill.

After slithering heart-stoppingly back and forward to within inches of the drop, the back wheels began to spin fruitlessly. The more Ivalin gunned the engine, the more the van settled in the mud.

It was time for a veteran of driving dumper trucks on muddy building sites and lorries down soggy country lanes in England to teach the off-road racer a trick or two. I grabbed a spade, went back up the track to find some dry, crumbly earth and spread it around the back wheels. Then I climbed on the roof of the Transit and jumped up and down and bellowed for Ivalin to gently reverse.

A little later and we are on our way back to the raspberry fields. I am trying not to look smug, and Ivalin is clearly not happy to have been got out of trouble by an English townie. His chagrin is obvious from the way he is driving even more madly than usual.

Nearing the bottom of the slope down to the river and

secret entrance into the forest, he guns the engine, hits something submerged in the stream and I take off from the passenger seat. It is only a few inches to the roof of the Transit, but my velocity is such that I am obviously going to make an impression on the thin, unlined metal sheeting. It is as if things are happening in slow motion as contact occurs and I slide into benign unconsciousness.

~

I have fallen foul of and broken the basic rule concerning finding and engaging the Forbidden Gear.

After treatment with a shot of *Rakia* and some sympathy from the Roma ladies, I was fully recovered from my encounter with the van roof. The pallets of raspberries were stacked in the cold room at Ivalin's factory, and I said goodbye to my new friends.

Having borrowed the Lada, I drove to Berkovitsa to pick up a bottle of good wine to go with dinner at Roger's house, then stopped off at the stork's nest on the outskirts of Komerinski. The happy event has occurred, and there are now four giant birds sharing the nest on the top of the post beyond the meat processing factory.

Thanks to the efforts of the keen amateur bird-watchers taking part in the most recent International White Stork Census, we know there are more than six thousand storks' nests in Bulgaria, most of which were occupied at the time of the count. Ironically and opposite to the dramatic decline in the human population, this denotes an increase in storks.

They really are an impressive sight in flight or at rest, and the mature adult can measure more than a metre from red beak tip to tail. Their wing span can reach more than two metres. Storks are carnivores and feed on insects, small mammals and fish, so the shallow river at Krasiva makes a perfect hunting ground for them. The youngsters are already the size of herring gulls and in another six weeks or so will fly the nest.

Having taken some photographs, I reached the luncheon club site and saw two members of the ladies dining club at the hikers' shelter. They flagged me down, and as I pulled over, a third member appeared. She was pushing a wheelbarrow which bore a dozen watermelons, almost cartoon-like in their bright greenness and monstrous size. Like birds and insects, bunches of grapes and spring onions, they obviously grow things bigger in rural Bulgaria.

The ladies would not take no for an answer in any language, and began loading the melons into the back of the Lada. The chassis settled lower on the wheels, and I realised the melons were a pay-back present for the box of English biscuits I dropped off yesterday. I shall have to be careful, as I am in danger of entering another Rural Present Loop. I have got stuck in this circle of politeness in other European countries, and it may apply in any rural area. It starts with a small gift of surplus vegetables, say a handful of courgettes, and custom demands a response. The giftee is then bound to return the compliment, most suitably with another species of fruit or vegetable. Returning the courgettes and pretending they are your own is not acceptable, and in fact considered an insult. In some remote villages, generational feuds have been started because of that sort of behaviour. The real problem with the Rural Present Loop comes when the receiver tries to outdo the giver in size and scale of the gift. It may start with an over-generous basket of pears, and end up with pigs, fields and even houses being resentfully presented to conform to the code.

As I had a case of wine on board, I pressed a bottle on them and it seems rude to refuse their invitation to try a glass.

Following a happy hour talking about our lives and family histories (I find wine makes intimate conversation possible in any language) I drove away, the boot of the

Lada almost scraping on the road. To gain momentum for the steep uphill drive, I put my foot down and went through the box and found the forbidden fifth gear.

Once stuck in it, I was unable to get out. The engine laboured ever more painfully as the hill got steeper, and then the inevitable happened. It stalled and died, we hiccupped to a stop, and I and the car and the watermelons and the gear were stuck.

~

Following the glow worm trail, I'm walking back from dinner at the very English home of Roger Smith. The only other guest was Ivailo Lazarov, and I think I know him better now.

Earlier, I had phoned Richard from the roadside to tell him about the gear problem, and within minutes a battered estate car screeched to a stop alongside.

The Moore's major domo gave me a withering look, and without speaking, brushed me aside, leapt into the driving seat and sent the Lada freewheeling back down the slope. Seconds from a sharp bend and a sheer drop, the engine caught and fired into life.

Like an exasperated parent with a stupid child, Ivo slowly repeated the warning about the fifth gear and said he would follow me to Roger's house in case I got into any more trouble in the half mile distance.

~

Apart from the post and rail fencing, the wigwams of runner beans and the British-registered cars outside, the converted barn overlooking the valley could be taken for a wealthy Bulgarian's holiday house. Inside, it could be nothing else but an Englishman's home, and a resolutely English Englishman's home.

The wedding-cake-icing plastered walls and ceiling of

the sitting room are painted in shades of magnolia and white. The room is large, but dominated by a monster flat-screen television. The comfortable sofa and dining suite are very British, and the paintings on the wall are of archetypal English landscapes. The kitchen is typically British, and the store cupboards and a back-up fridge are packed with British delicacies from Marmite to Cheddar cheese, proper marmalade and jams, and even McDougal's finest flour. Roger is an accomplished cook and baker, and says Bulgarian flour will just not give the desired result. Overall and fragrantly underlined by the smell of roasting lamb, his home is a celebration and a cocoon of Britishness.

Those of classic *bien-pensant* and *Guardian*-reading persuasion contemptuously mock Britons who take their Britishness with them when they move abroad. They sneer at expats pining for proper bacon and hard cheese, and say they should integrate and adapt and become part of the culture they have chosen to join. It is a deep irony that these same middle-class and middle-brow snobs actively encourage people who come to live in Britain from foreign parts to do exactly what Roger is doing, which is maintain their cultural habits and customs and preferences.

~

Opinions divide sharply with regard to the importance of luck or self-determination in how our lives turn out. Those who get what they seek in material terms tend to say that the harder they work the luckier they become. Others blame fate or fortune and are in good company with some of our greatest authors and philosophers and religions.

After several decades of wrestling with the possible alternatives, I have come to the conclusion that what happens to us and what we become is a mixture of luck and circumstance and ambition and determination. Unlike Forest Gump, I don't believe that life is like a box of chocolates, but rather a game of cards. You have no say in the hands you are given, but the way you play them can make all the difference.

I do, though, think there are some people who are genuinely unlucky in non life-threatening ways, and that Roger Smith is one. Tonight he talked freely of the ups and downs in his life, and without a shred of self-pity or attempt to blame anyone for a string of misfortunes and setbacks that would suggest he has smashed more mirrors and crossed the paths or more black cats than most, particularly in affairs of the heart. But he has at least had an interesting life so far.

After a career as a sea-going cook, his first marriage lasted nine months. His second did better, but ended when his wife ran off with their son's best friend. He then met a lady on the World Wide Web, wooed and won her from the wealthy owner of a *château* in France. She suggested they set up a restaurant to take advantage of Roger's skills, but of all the villages and towns in France they chose to buy one where the mayor was the proprietor of the nearest competition. As anyone who knows about French mayors and their power, this was never going to be a good idea.

When his third life partner disappeared from his life, Roger found himself with severely reduced funds. Liking the sound of Bulgarian property prices, he toured the country and settled on the derelict barn with the fabulous views.

He camped next to the building and set to work making a home with his own hands and some professional help. After months of work, he was away in England when thieves arrived. Knowing they would not be disturbed, they removed some roof tiles to get in, and spent weeks feasting on the contents of the property. Domestic appliances, furniture and even solar panels were taken, and Roger came home to an apparently intact house which had been virtually gutted.

Then he heard that because it had been an outbuilding, his new home was not and could not be officially registered. He also learned that a local farmer was going to build a factory next door. As it turned out, this was actually a stroke of good luck as the farmer was Ivalin and the factory more of a storage place for his fruit harvests.

~

The roast lamb with five veg might not be everyone's idea of an ideal meal in temperatures in the 30s, but it was delicious. During the long evening and excellent dinner, I also learned a little about Ivo.

Warmed by a glass or two of wine, he became almost affable, and I learned he lives in Berkovitsa, and served in the army, rather than I had suspected when we first met, the Bulgarian equivalent of the KGB. I am also almost sure he has been my guardian angel in matters where I could have fallen foul of the Berkovitsa police force.

Like many of his countrymen, Ivo is not pleased with the way the population is shrinking as the Roma community grows, or that his grandfather had his properties taken away by the communists.

He is unmarried and has a girlfriend who works in a distant land, and is clearly highly intelligent and informed about his country's history. He is also passionately patriotic. I think he does not resent foreigners bringing their money to Bulgaria, but is full of anger at the wrong choices his country has made and the situation he and it is in because of them.

A rustling on the other side of the lane brings my attention back to the moment, and I swing the beam of my torch across to a gap in the hedgerow. A pair of eyes glow greenly in the light and regard me unwinkingly. They are set too low to belong to a human or a bear, and I think a fox or wolf would have reacted to the light and made off. I suspect it is one of the Krasiva Night Chorus, come to remind me that the members will be expecting a full Bulgarian breakfast come morning.

In Bulgaria, yogurt is considered to be an indispensable mainstay of the national cuisine. It not only tastes good, but is regarded as highly medicinal in its qualities. To increase its richness, it is often strained before being used. The traditional way is to put yogurt into cheesecloth and twist it in to a tight ball. The top of the cheesecloth is tied and the ball suspended overnight. It is taken as a *meze* or appetiser, and, though local variations may occur, this is the traditional recipe.

Таратор
Tarator
(Chilled yogurt and cucumber soup)

Ingredients

Three cucumbers, finely diced
Two cups of plain yogurt
Half a cup of ground walnuts
Three cloves of crushed garlic
Some dill, finely chopped
A quarter of a cup of sunflower oil
A good pinch of salt

Method

1. Beat the yogurt
2. Add the garlic, walnuts, cucumber, oil and salt
3. Dilute with some water
4. Stir and serve, topped with dill

We say kebab, the Turks and Bulgarians say 'kebap'. We usually think of it as slices of lamb in a pitta bread wrap, and you will find somewhere serving takeaway Doner Kebaps in every sizeable town in Bulgaria. The term actually means small pieces of meat, often in a sort of stew. This is one of five variations on a theme, and is made with pork:

Кавърма Кебар
Kavarma Kebap
(Kebab)

Ingredients

Half a cup of olive oil
A kilo of cubed pork
Four chopped leeks
A tablespoon of tomato paste
A teaspoon of paprika
Half a chopped onion
Salt to taste
Black pepper
Half a cup of water
Half a cup of chicken stock
Some chopped parsley

Method

1. Heat the oil in a heavy pan and fry the pork till brown
2. Remove the pork and add the leeks
3. Cook the leeks well and then add the paprika, tomato paste, salt and pepper
4. Add the water and the stock and mix well
5. Re-add the pork

6. Turn the heat down and simmer uncovered to reduce
7. Sprinkle the parsley and chopped onion over before serving

I have always thought that there's not much you can do to a pumpkin to make it taste good except making a thick soup and adding lots and lots of cream. Since making and trying this recipe, I have changed my mind:

печено тиква с мед и орехи
Pecheno tikva s med i orekhi
(roast pumpkin and honey with walnuts)

Ingredients

A small pumpkin
Two tablespoons of sugar
A teaspoon of cinnamon
Half a teaspoon of nutmeg
Half a teaspoon of allspice
A quarter teaspoon of cloves
150g of crushed walnuts
Four teaspoons of honey

Method

1. Pre-heat oven to 200°C
2. Cut pumpkin into small uniform blocks*, leaving the peel on
3. Combine the sugar, cinnamon, nutmeg, allspice and cloves in a bowl and mix well
4. Fill a baking tray with water to cover the bottom
5. Dip each side of the pumpkin blocks into the spice mix and rub into all exposed surfaces
6. Put them skin side down into the baking tray and cover with foil
7. Roast for half an hour or so till the blocks are fork tender

8. Uncover the blocks and roast for another ten minutes to caramelise the tops
9. Add honey to the tops and cover with walnuts before serving

*Use the leftover pieces of pumpkin for soup and roast the seeds for nibbles
You may also wish to add raisins and more sugar to the top of the blocks

На къщата
On the house

House flies: 237
Horse flies: 89
Wasps: 13
Other: 11

I don't know the useful life of a sheet of flypaper but mine will soon need changing. This is not because mine are losing their fatal attraction but because there will soon be no space between corpses and the sticky surface is beginning to look like the inside of an Eccles cake.

The flypaper may be a success story, but I have become the victim of a protection racket.

Храни куче, да те лае is a catchy old Bulgarian proverb along the lines of 'Feed a dog to bark at you' and I now know what it means.

I came out of the house in a hurry the other day and forgot Muttley's breakfast. He made no comment but raised an eyelid in a somehow menacing way as I passed, and the night chorus kicked off for the first time in a week.

The next morning I left the house carrying a piece of his favourite smoked sausage, and found he had company. Standing on either side of him were a whippet with anorexia and what looked like a cross between a great dane and a dachshund. They said nothing, just regarding me balefully until I returned to the house and fetched some more sausage.

Last night was blissfully silent throughout the valley. As the sausage is so expensive I shall try a pig's head tomorrow. If it does not meet the standards of the racketeers I shall go to Montana and buy a shipping order of sausage at Lidl's. It will not be cheap, but an unbroken night's sleep will make it good value.

~

I am en route to Roger's to thank him for last night's food and entertainment, and to drop off a box of baklava and some British sweets for my Roma friends.

It is the end of the working week, and Ivalin is paying his pickers. There is an almost festive mood as the ladies take their ease around the table in the yard and their employer begins what has obviously become a pleasant ritual.

Ivalin sits at the head of the table and refers to his ledger, calling out each woman's name in order of seniority, telling her how much she has earned and then solemnly paying the notes and coins into her hand. There is no round of applause after each announcement, but it has that sort of benevolent, prize-day feeling.

Some of the girls do better than others, but it looks to me as if most of his team are getting the equivalent of around fifty pounds for the week's work. It doesn't sound a lot, but I know it's more than the going rate for most fruit and vegetable pickers in the region. That's why so many casual farm labourers come to Britain from this end of Europe when they hear about how comparatively high the pay is. Of course, they either do not know or do not care that the cost of living is much, much higher there, and many pickers go home wiser and no richer.

Before leaving, I stand and read out a speech Ivalin has coached me in. According to him, it thanks the ladies for their company and friendship, and concludes with a joke about my lack of skill as a fruit picker. I don't expect a round of polite applause as I sit down, but am surprised at the complete silence. The looks of bewilderment suggests my pronunciation has been awry. The pretty young woman looks at me and then asks Ivalin a question. He fires off a burst of joined-up words, and the Roma girls collapse in fits of laughter. Then Donka holds up her hand, makes a fist and then lifts her little finger up and waggles it. This is the signal for more pantomimed hilarity. I shall never know exactly what the joke was, but it was obviously at my expense, and some sign language is international.

~

This morning we will be looking at three houses in the village which Ivo says are definitely for sale. They are empty and available because the former occupants have died, and the relevant relatives have agreed that their homes be sold. This would be almost a normal course of events in much of the rest of Europe, but the situation is not always so straightforward in Bulgaria, particularly in rural areas.

When a will has been properly drawn up and notarised it is usually plain sailing, but in the case of intestacy things can get complicated. With various codicils and when there is no surviving spouse, the law requires that the estate should be divided amongst all the children, including any adoptees. When there is property involved, all the beneficiaries must agree to its sale, and to the asking price, and how much it can be reduced to close a sale. This can lead to family fall-outs, and Ivo knows of properties that have lain empty and unsold until all the original inheritors have died.

There are no such problems with the properties we will be looking at, and we are starting with a house just across the lane from Ivalin's headquarters. There is a padlock on a rusty chain keeping the gate shut, and I feel a familiar tingle of anticipation and curiosity as Ivo turns the key.

I have looked at and written about hundreds of properties for sale in France and elsewhere in Europe and have even bought a few, yet I still get excited and enthused at the prospect of nosing around old rural buildings. I think the attraction is partly the excuse for looking into other people's lives and how they lived, and the chance to consider how the place could be transformed into a characterful and functional home. Not having to come up with the money and actually do the work makes it even more enjoyable.

Regardless of how beguiling are the homes we are viewing today, I shall not be putting in any offers. I have promised my wife to not even think about the attractions of a holiday home in the Balkans, and resist the temptation of being able to buy a whole house with a credit card with a modest limit.

In estate agency terms of reference, the 1950's communist replacement house is on the wrong side of the lane as it does not directly overlook the valley, but there will be wonderful views from the top floor.

The grey cement rendered, shabby and box-like building stands on a triangular spit of land just off the lane, with a track alongside leading up past some small vineyards to a forest on the upper slopes. The garden is totally overgrown, but there are fruit trees, a vine and evidence of a former vegetable plot. A string of dried peppers stretches between the washing line posts, and the remains of the original cottage sit gently decaying next to the sentry-box earth closet.

As with all the communist cubes, concrete steps lead up to the first floor living area. We start at ground level, where there are three rooms with interconnecting doors and very small windows through which little light filters. Ivo says that in the old days and when whole families shared a house like this, this part of the house would be used for sleeping. Each of the rooms would hold at least two beds, and the tiny windows prevented loss of heat. As he says, the thinking then was that you went to bed to sleep, so light was not necessary or even desirable.

Before we leave the ground floor, Ivo shows us what would have been a state-of-the-art shower system when the property was built. It is the same sort of device as Elenko and other villagers still use to heat water for washing and bathing. The rusty metal cylinder has copper and steel pipes running from and to it; one rises vertically to the ceiling, where it ends with an unexpectedly elegant swan neck and large metal rose to spray the water out. Ivo says the device was in regular use until the occupant died a couple of months ago. He sneaks a look to see my reaction, and I score a small point by saying the heater is a luxury compared to the tin bath our family bathed in every Friday when I was a child.

Outside, the open concrete steps lead up to a landing, from where the old wooden door gives on to a passageway and three rooms. All contain furniture and furnishings which look about the same age as the house. The largest room looks out and across the lane and there are views of the mountains through a clump of trees on the opposite verge. It is a large and well-lit room, lined with patterned wallpaper. The room is furnished with a pair of upright chairs and a heavy post-war table with sugar-twist legs. In one corner is a small table on which sits a television set of the same era as the house.

The next room was obviously used as a kitchen, and holds a well-scrubbed table, its surface scarred by decades of score marks. Shelving lines one whitewashed wall, and by the window is a familiar and nostalgic sight. It is a tall, plastic-veneered kitchen cabinet with frosted glass doors at the top, and a hinged drop-down leaf to use as a work surface. In my childhood there were few homes without what almost ranked as a fitted kitchen.

Like the floor of the sitting room, the wooden planking is covered by squares of linoleum and what look like home-made woollen rugs.

The third and smallest room looks out towards the track and the rows of small vineyards and, beyond them, the upper forest. There is a bed with a small wicker table next to it, and a large wooden cross fixed to the wall above. A monumental wardrobe reaches almost to the ceiling, and in one corner is a chest of drawers with a delicate and intricate lace runner on top. On the runner stands a cracked ewer and jug, and an old monochrome photograph in a plastic frame. It shows a tall, thin young man, standing stiffly upright next to a seated figure. He is wearing a heavy, three-piece suit and his thick dark hair has been plastered down and parted almost in the middle. He looks uncomfortable in the unaccustomed collar and tie, which seem to be keeping his head rigidly erect. One large and already gnarled hand holds on to the narrow lapel of his jacket, and the other rests almost tentatively on the shoulder of the beautiful girl sitting in the straight-backed chair.

Looking at the couple, I think how casually we accept these frozen fractions of time. This man and his wife lived their lives and were together here, and now there is nothing left of them but this reminder of another time.

Turning to leave, I see a door half-hidden behind the massive wardrobe. Thinking it might lead to a closet or even another room, I walk over and tug at the Bakelite handle. Nothing happens and I realise I have been pulling when I should have been pushing. I give a hefty shove, the door gives way, and I find myself teetering on the edge of a sheer drop to the yard below.

Strong hands grasp me from behind, and I am returned to safety by my guardian angel. He tells me I should be more careful in strange surroundings. I tell him that, after half a lifetime of exploring ancient houses and writing about them, I am still a sucker for a closed door.

~

On our way to the next viewing we stop to pick plums from a roadside tree, and Ivo says that next month there is a festival in a nearby town dedicated to the fruit, *Rakia* made from it, and even the Bulgarian version of Turkish Delight. Next week there's a fete of watermelons, a convention for bagpipe players and a gathering of gold prospectors I might want to attend. He adds that it is said there is some cause for celebration every day of the year in Bulgaria, but two reasons for feeling miserable. I say I like the sound of panning for gold and the watermelon festival, but may give a miss to the bagpipe convention.

We sit in the sun and look out across the valley and enjoy our wild breakfast. Ivo asks if I liked the house, and says the owner is asking around 11,000 leva (£5000), which he thinks is too much. The man says the price is high because all the fixtures and fittings are included in the sale.

Sally says that whoever buys it will need to make sure that the furniture is included in the contract. She thought she and Richard had bought everything in their first house in Krasiva, but woke up a month later to find the previous owner standing by the bed, which she said she had come to take away with all the other furniture.

~

The next house on our itinerary is across the lane and two doors away from where I am staying in the guest house.

It is almost identical to the one we have just looked at and in about the same condition. The garden is bigger, but slopes steeply downhill into the valley and is so overgrown as to be inaccessible. In its favour, Sally points out that the people here are past masters at growing things on hill slopes. Ivo says that the jungle of weed and bramble has taken over after just one summer's neglect, and hides a small vineyard and orchard from which it is said the owners made the finest wine and preserves in the area.

The ground floor is far below the level of the lane and through a tunnel of foliage, but worth the effort of climbing through it. Illuminated by oil lamps and the light from one window, I can see the cellar is filled with wonderful things. In the centre of the single room is a row of old oak barrels which Ivo says contain many litres of vintage *Rakia*. One wall is taken up entirely by a racking system bearing hundreds of bottles of home-made wine. Two other walls are lined with shelving on which sit dozens of preserve jars and wide-necked bottles. I walk along the row and see peach and pear and plum and walnut and all manner of other fruit, and some things I did not know could be preserved. On the fourth wall is a very large and old cupboard, locked with a chain and padlock. Ivo does not know what is in it, but says there are all sorts of rumours in the village.

As we leave, he explains that the furniture upstairs goes with the sale, but not the contents of the barrels and bottles or the mysterious cupboard. He adds that it was recently announced that the heart of the former magistrate of Berkovitsa and famous writer Ivan Vazov had been found preserved in a jar. Perhaps, he says with a deadpan face, other bits of the rest of the great man might be under lock and key in the cellar of this very house. Or as the more scurrilous rumours allege, they may be the last remains of the former master of the house.

~

Now this is something *completely* different.

The roughly-rendered outer walls are snow-white, set off by the rich terra cotta of the roof tiles. It is the first house I have seen with curved Mediterranean 'boot' tiles.

The single-storey building sits comfortably on a level plane overlooking the valley, and the view from the earth closet discreetly placed behind the building would make you want to use it with the door open. The reason the house is for sale is made clear by the two death notices taped to the gate.

Unusually, the cottage is surrounded by flower beds as well as fruit and vegetable gardens, and sits like an island in a sea of fecundity. Rows of sweet corn line the winding path, huge bunches of purple grapes threaten to break free of restraint and cascade down on to the porch and the onion sets and tomatoes could be growing in a land of giants.

And there is more. Side-on to the lane and with equally breath-taking views of the valley and mountains beyond is an old barn of ancient red brick laced with weathered oak beams.

The wonderful old building obviously escaped the attentions of the communist cubists, and is every dreamer's idea of an idyllic period country cottage. I trace the outline of the credit card holder in my back pocket, then follow Ivo, Richard and Sally through the rustic gate.

~

In a yard at the back of the cottage, a small man with a big axe is working at a log pile. Above and behind him, smoke curls lazily from the chimney. I wonder at the idea of needing a fire on a broiling summer day, then a delicious aroma from the open door reminds me that Krasiva stoves are used for cooking as well as heating.

The man nods affably, then comes over and shakes my hand before Ivo begins the introductions. I have been warned this will happen. It is not because the man thinks he knows me, but because it is an old country custom to greet the most senior member of the party first. A burst of Bulgarian follows, and Ivo says we are being invited in to look around; there is also some simple food if we can stay to eat. As the man leads the way through the plank door, Ivo says he is the son-in-law of the couple who lived here for more than fifty years. The wife died two months ago, and the husband followed her within a week. It was as if he did not want to carry on on his own.

Inside, two women stand at a stove, and, if it were not for their clothing, we could be time travellers.

The compacted earth floor has a slight sheen from decades of use, and is covered in places with tasselled, woven carpets. The walls of the large room are the same brilliant white as the outside, which enhances the light coming through the two small, shoulder-high windows.

One of the walls is lined with wooden shelving from which hang a variety of heavy pots and pans. The chimney breast is of stone, and probably built so massively to help take the weight of the roof. As Ivo said before we arrived, the cottage walls are made from mud. Or rather, earth mixed with straw and the droppings of goats and cows and sheep. This way of using readily available materials for building work is thousands of years old, and makes for surprisingly strong and completely waterproof walls.

Curiously, the stove is not on the hearth, but in the middle of the room with a metal flue pipe running into the chimney. As Sally points out, this keeps the heat in the room and even the pipe would act as a form of radiator.

A big black pot bubbles on the combination of heating stove and cooking range, which is the size and shape of a low sideboard. It is very hot in the room, and I imagine it could be quite comfortable when the snow lies deep outside.

Apart from the women's dress, the only clue we have not time-travelled to an earlier century is the single unshaded light bulb hanging from the ceiling.

Another burst of Bulgarian, and we smile and incline our heads in the correct direction as the older of the two ladies uses a ladle to invite us to explore.

We choose the left-hand door, stepping around two big slabs of what looks like marble and entering a room about half the size of the main living area. It too is dominated by a centrally-sited stove, and near it and against one wall is a double, iron-framed bed. It is covered with a patchwork quilt, and I suspect it is where the couple spent their nights for more than fifty years.

On the wall opposite is a wooden framework with a ceramic bowl let into it at about waist height. There is a single tap above it, so the house has some form of piped running water. The earth floor is mostly covered with a large, patterned carpet, and there is a utility-era wardrobe and sideboard on the wall with a window looking out across the valley.

I stand and try to imagine what the life of the couple has been like, and how often they left the village. In our world, we think we need 24/7 access to shops and online sources for all the things we think we need. Here, the couple would have been living on and mostly from the earth.

The third room lies on the other side of the chimney breast, and after a caution from the younger woman, Ivo knocks before we enter.

There is the same type of monumental stove dominating the room, and two single beds stand against the longer walls. Alongside one is an old sideboard, and on it a small, very modern television set. Next to it, a mobile phone is blinking to show it is receiving a charge, so there is at least one electrical point in the house. The television is showing some sort of pop programme, and watching it from the nearest bed is a young girl. She has a tiny dog cradled in her arms, and gets up as we stand awkwardly by the stove. She is clearly very self-possessed, and not put out to find a quartet of foreigners arriving in her bedroom.

She talks with Ivo for a while, and he explains that she is the daughter of the younger woman and has come with the family from Sofia to see her grandparent's house for possibly the last time. The television and phone are hers, he adds rather unnecessarily. She speaks some English, and is happy to practice on us. She takes over at his invitation, and explains that her name is Silviya, which means 'from the forest', though she actually lives with her parents. She is at college and working hard on her English to help with her career. It is no surprise to learn that her ambition is to live and work in England.

A voice calls from the living room, and Silviya says the food is ready. We follow her in the direction of the piquant aroma, and I think how almost incredibly people's lives have changed in the half-century since her grandparents moved into the house. The changes are further exemplified by the television and phone and Silviya's plans for the future, and are magnified a hundredfold by their setting in a place where things have changed so little in a long lifetime.

~

We are sitting in the hiker's hut next to the village shop, which is no more than two hundred yards from the mud house. Ivo has driven off to see how his team are progressing with a job in Berkovitsa, and has left us to talk about what we have seen.

Before leaving he said that the old house was just as solid as the two communist cubes, but would be more expensive to work on for obvious reasons. He would come up with some estimates for updating the cottage and repairing the roof of the barn, which could at least treble the asking price of five thousand leva.

Although I have been banned from buying even an almost literally dirt-cheap house, it is good to imagine what could be done with the cottage to make it habitable while retaining its old-world appeal. I start to talk about concreting over the mud floors and installing a kitchen and bathroom, but Sally has another, much better idea.

If it were her choice, she would leave the mud house almost as it is and would concentrate on the barn. The roof could be fixed and the brickwork and beams restored, and the first floor made into an open-plan living area. There could be a high-tech corner kitchen and a bathroom with a toilet and power shower, and, best of all, the whole of the rotting side facing the valley could be replaced with floor-to-ceiling windows. It would make a superb writer or artist's retreat with its combination of ancient and modern and the spiritual ambience of the mud house standing exactly as it had done for two hundred years. The whole project would cost less than a beach hut in a down-market English resort, and the only problem for a writer like me would be having the willpower to pull the blinds over the windows in the barn to mask the amazing views and get down to work.

I open my mouth to come up with a list of objections, and realise I can't think of any.

I have come here to write about an apparently bonkers scheme to breathe life back into a dying village, and after seeing only three properties I am sold on the idea of owning a house made of mud.

~

No glow worms or fireflies to light me to my bed tonight, but the cloudless sky is ablaze with stars and the moon is full. This may account for my mad desire to buy a house made of earth, animal poo and pee.

We talked long over dinner at Sally and Richard's home, and they could see what was going on in my mind and heart. They have made no attempt to recruit me to be part of their artistic community, but could see the struggle between infatuation and practicality. Then, over a last glass of plum *Rakia*, they made me an offer which was more than generous. To ensure nobody else bought the mud house and ruined it by improving it, they would buy it. They would also set Ivo to converting the barn. If I and my wife were in accord sometime in the future, they would sell us the property at what it had cost them to buy and restore.

I hear a low growl as I arrive at the guest house, throw Muttley a chicken leg and put my finger to my lips. Then after saying goodnight to the looming outline of Kom, I think about the attractions of having a home here, and how it could just be possible that my hosts' dream of bringing new life to a dying village could become a reality.

Time out

There are twelve official public holidays in Bulgaria. They include a day off in March to mark the liberation from Turkish rule in 1878. The first of May is International Workers' Day, the sixth of May is St George's Day, and on the 24th there is a day off to celebrate Saint Cyril and his brother Methodius. The sixth of September is Unification Day, and the 22nd is Independence Day. There's also a National Awakening Day on the first day of November.

Apart from fetes or gatherings to celebrate various fruits, vegetables and hobbies, non-public excuses for celebration include saints 'name days'. The original tradition was that, on a saint's day, guests would pitch up uninvited at the home of someone named for that saint. It would then be his or her duty to ply the arrivals with food and drink. Nowadays, the tradition has been amended to the name-bearer taking his friends out for a meal. As there are more than 150 saints' days in the Bulgarian calendar, it means good business for restaurants and bars.

Property matters

As touched on earlier, many properties in villages in the Montana region stay empty after the death of their owners for purely practical reasons.

Apart from the inheritors having to agree on an asking price, the value may be so low that it is literally not worth the time and travel costs to visit the area and sign the necessary documents.

There is also the problem of lack of availability of documentation because of the chaotic aftermath of communism. This has brought in its wake all sorts of complications that do not apply in a country with a less troubled history in regard to public and private ownership.

Because of the lack of records concerning who owns or owned what, it might be necessary for two neighbours to swear an affidavit that the vendor is a relative of the deceased and thus a possible inheritor of the property.

Then there's the muddle surrounding the deliciously intriguingly-named *skitsa*. This is a cadastral plan giving information on the boundaries and must be no more than six months out of date when used in property exchange. If this law were applied to the letter it would be a problem in Krasiva, as the village *skitsa* has not been updated since the 1930s.

There are other requirements on the seller and buyer, which make it seem surprising that any rural properties ever change hands.

In fact it is usually a much smoother process than the above would suggest, especially if you have someone like Ivo Lazarov to take care of the negotiations and visits to the Town Hall and generally steer you through the process.

The delicious aroma issuing from the mud house came from roasted peppers. The Bulgarians say it is the smell of late summer and autumn. The ladies had done them on the top of the cooking range and added them to a simple salad. This treatment is a bit more complicated, but really worth the effort:

Чушки Бюрек
Chushki Bjurek
Byurek peppers

Ingredients

Eight red peppers (the long and pointy sweet ones)
Four eggs
180g of feta-type cheese
A clove of garlic, minced
Some vegetable oil
Some plain yogurt

and for the batter

Two eggs
Six tablespoons of plain flour
Six tablespoons of breadcrumbs

Method

1. Roast the peppers (preferably on a Bulgarian cooking range, but a barbie or oven will do)
2. Cook till almost charred in places and turn over and repeat the process
3. Let them cool and then peel and de-seed
4. Break one egg in a bowl and beat till it foams
5. Crumble the cheese and add to the egg mixture with the minced garlic
6. Stuff your peppers gently

7. Beat the other egg for the batter
8. Roll each pepper in flour, then egg, then breadcrumbs
9. Fry in the oil, turning once
10. Serve piping hot with a dollop of yogurt (I like to add a little paprika to the yogurt)

Continuing the vegetarian theme, this simple and simply delicious potato 'pie' is said to originate in the Rhodopes mountain range area:

пататник
patatnik
(potato pie)

Ingredients

A kg of potatoes
One large onion
Three teaspoons of dried thyme
Some vegetable oil
Some seasoning

Method

1. Peel and grate the potatoes
2. Sprinkle with salt and set aside
3. Strain the grated potatoes
4. Grate the onion and mix with potato and the thyme
5. Heat the oil in a pan and add the mixture, spreading to make a thickness of about a centimetre
6. Cover, cook till golden brown, then turn your potato pie over and repeat the process

My mother always said that the first word I spoke was 'semolina.' I have been a fan ever since. This is real comfort food stuff and fairly heavy on calories, but so what:

грис халва
gris halva
(semolina pudding)

Ingredients

A cup of semolina flour
A cup of sugar
A cup of water
A quarter of a cup of butter
Some oil
A tablespoon of vanilla extract
Some crushed hazel or walnuts
Some cinnamon

Method

1. In a saucepan, boil the water and sugar and vanilla
2. In another pan, heat the oil and add the butter and semolina
3. Be careful not to burn the flour and simmer for at least ten minutes
4. When the semolina flour mix is cooked, add gradually to the water and sugar mix and simmer
5. When there are no lumps and it starts separating from the pan, it is ready for the final step
6. Spread the mix in a greased baking sheet to around two centimetres thickness, sprinkle with the nuts and cinnamon and allow to cool and firm up before serving in chunky slices. It is nice with custard or yogurt or even cream

Разходка в гората
A walk in the woods

A dramatic summer storm during the night.

The furious downpour drummed on the roof and windows, and great sheets of fire lit up the valley, but it was somehow comforting to lie safely inside watching nature at work. When I came out on to the balcony this morning, all was fresh and green. The deluge had also cleared the air and brought the ragged line of the Planina range into even sharper focus.

I took the flypapers down earlier, and will see if I can do without them. It is not that I am the sort of person who would not harm a fly, but that the hundreds of rotting corpses are an unpleasant sight and a constant reminder of how brief life can be before we all come to a sticky end. I also found a beautiful, long-legged and crimson-winged insect struggling to escape in the living room yesterday. When I tried to release it, the wings came away in my hand and I had to kill it. Strange that we should care more about attractive creatures than ugly ones, but such is the illogicality of the human race.

I gave the dead legions a fairly respectable burial in the garden then prepared the equipment for my attempt to reach Berkovitsa the hard way. I am assured by Ivalin that it is no more than three miles across country and through the forests, and some villagers do the return trip to market every week. He added that all I would need was a good compass and to keep an eye out for wild pigs, bears, wolves, foxes and brigands.

I think he was joking, but will be taking my clasp knife and staff for protection. I have a small plastic compass which came free as part of a promotion at my local garage, but I don't think it is reliable. When I tried it in the garden it showed true North to lie in three completely different positions. It would anyway be of not much use without a suitable map, and the best one I have shows little more than the main roads and tourist attractions in the whole country. I also have an aerial map of this area, but it is an American Air Force chart used by navigators on bombing raids over Bulgaria during World War II. Richard says he bought a hand-held GPS tracking device at Montana market last year, but the instructions are in Chinese. Despite the lack of technical equipment, I am sure I will not have a navigational problem as Berkovitsa lies virtually at the foot of Kom.

I have a small rucksack, and will take emergency provisions of a couple of high-energy Marmite and peanut butter sandwiches and a packet of Maltesers. I will also take a flask of coffee, a torch, a tube of sun cream and a couple of books. One will be *A Short Walk in the Hindu Kush*. Eric Newby is a master of travel writing and a literary hero of mine, and a few pages of his work can give me inspiration when I am stuck for a word or passage. The most common question readers ask me is how I think of things to write about when in a foreign land, and I always say the trick is of choosing things *not* to write about. When we parted company, my then agent and publisher said they thought I made some very bad choices.

~

So far so good.

It's been downhill all the way and I have reached the stream without incident. Fences were not replaced at the end of the communist era because nobody was sure where the boundaries between public and private property lay, so the countryside is wide open. From the bottom of the valley I can still see the roof of the guest house on the skyline, but have taken the time to make a giant arrow from broken branches pointing towards it. This is just in case I do not return until after dark or become disoriented, and was the first tip in my copy of *Fieldcraft and Foraging for Boy Scouts* (1959): *always mark the way you came so you know where to return.*

I now have to either walk along the course of the stream and try to skirt the forest, or forge straight ahead into its dark depths. I can see no pathway, and the secret passage we followed in Ivalin's van is a mile or so to the west. In any case, being secret I would not know where to look for it.

I toss a mental coin and decide to follow the river.

~

The trouble with rivers is that they take the easy way out and follow the line of least resistance. This one is no exception, and has disappeared into the forest, leaving me another choice to have to make. Shall I follow it into the dark heart of Tanglewood, or follow my instincts and the sun?

I decide on the latter, but there is a problem. We all know the sun rises in the east and sets in the west, but it doesn't seem to be going anywhere at the moment. I take out my compass and watch the needle swing and tremble and then settle. I know Berkovitsa lies due south of the village, so decide to walk in the direction indicated. But before leaving the river, I construct another arrow pointing the way I came, and commit any remarkable features of the landscape to memory.

~

It is getting hotter, and the sun seems to have moved little. I don't know what time it is as I left my mobile phone on the table when I was packing supplies in the rucksack. I wish I had brought water instead of coffee, which my fieldcraft book says is dehydrating, but anyway take a cup and eat all the Maltesers for an energy boost. There are no tracks or signs of civilisation and not even an occasional plane passes overhead. Either side are long, rocky ridges and I am at the bottom of a great trench of sparse grass broken by copses of small trees and outcrops of veined blue-grey stone. All is very still and the sound of my breathing is magnified as I slog on. Around me a profusion of wild flowers and plants, and ahead on the track I spot a small patch of blue. It is a rubber glove, and it gives me heart to know that Man has walked this way before.

~

An hour later, and the features of the landscape have not changed. I am still in the grassy defile, skirting the edge of the great forest which lies between Krasiva and Berkovitsa. But the stream has reappeared, just yards inside the forest. It looks very inviting and at least I know I shall not die of thirst. I believe this could be the stream which runs south through the forest and then through the suburbs of Berkovitsa, but of course it could be another one, heading the opposite way.

Seeking shelter from the merciless sun, I sit with my back against a rock and think what it must have been like for T E Lawrence when he crossed the implacable Nefud desert to attack Aqaba. To take my mind off my fears, I reach for one of the books in my rucksack. It is Bad Land by Jonathan Raban, and I have reached the part where he finds an abandoned schoolhouse in the vast and empty reaches of Montana, the namesake of this province of Bulgaria. Coincidentally, Raban quotes from a text book advising children on how to act if they become lost in the wilderness of the American Montana. Though in another country, I read the passage carefully:

> If you ever find you are lost, do not become frightened. There is more danger in fright than there is of starvation or accident. If you allow yourself to become frightened you become possessed of what we call 'the panic of the lost'.
>
> As soon as you discover you have lost your way in the wilderness, sit down with your back against a stump or stone, take out your jack-knife and play mumblety-peg or sing a song. This will pull you together, so to speak. Then take a stick, smooth off a place in the dirt, and try to map out your wanderings. Making this map will cause you to remember forgotten objects you have passed on the road and may help you to retrace your steps.

I always carry a jack-knife when in the wilderness, but do not know how to play mumblety-peg. I could sing a song, but my throat is very dry and I don't want to attract the wrong sort of attention if, as Ivalin says, here there be wolves and even bears in the dark depths of the forest. It would be hard for any town dweller who has never been lost in the countryside to understand the fear that grips ones innards when you finally admit to yourself that you don't know where you are. I am only a couple of miles from civilisation, but it is quite possible that I could wander in this great valley for days on end... or even to the end of my days.

~

Much of my childhood was spent watching low-budget war movies, which often featured plucky Brits fighting their way through the impenetrable rain forests of Burma, usually led by Errol Flynn pretending to be English. Now, I have an inkling of what it must have been like in real life.

At least the Chindits had their machetes and jungle fatigues; I have my clasp knife and am wearing a vest, long shorts and trainers. I'm bleeding from a dozen minor wounds, and finding the going hard. There will be no human enemy lurking in wait for me, but I have heard strange sounds.

Most people's idea of a forest is a place where there are lots of trees, mostly a respectable distance apart. There will be a myriad of paths between them, and a bed of dead leaves to walk on.

This forest begs to differ. It is like something from an animated Disney film, and a dark and forbidding place. The trees are so close their branches seem to intertwine, and beneath my feet snake-like roots lie in waiting. There are saplings and bushes growing right down to the edge of the stream, so I have taken to walking in it. This is not easy, as the way is barred by fallen trunks and branches, and the bed is a mass of gravel and sharp stones.

The Germans have a word for nearly everything, and it is usually a long one. *Waldeinsamkeit* is the feeling of being at one with a forest. If I knew where I was, I think I could feel at one with nature here, but fear overcomes my philosophy. A little earlier I rested on the bank and heard the cracking of dry wood, then a snuffle and a grunt. I saw nothing, but imagined much.

~

I am safely home, and will have a tale to tell my grandchildren.

I failed in my mission to reach Berkovitsa by the forest

route, but I did find Ivalin's secret raspberry fields. The stream led me to the tiny bridge with the plaque in remembrance of his mother, and from there I followed the track to the clearing and then the open lands below the village. As I laboured uphill, bleeding from my wounds and all but exhausted, I was overtaken by an elderly lady. She smiled as she passed and said something which sounded encouraging. She was carrying a shopping bag which appeared full, so it is quite possible that she was returning from a walk to the market at Berkovitsa. Fortunately for my sense of dignity, I was not able to ask.

На скалите
On the rocks

Only twenty miles on the clock, but we've already passed or even been overtaken by three cars towing others like impatient mothers dragging their tardy children.

I wonder aloud if this is a way of saving on fuel, and Ivo grunts his acknowledgement of the jibe. Then he says the Bulgarian breakdown service is too expensive for most people. Many drivers carry a length of rope in the car to help strangers get home. It also comes in useful if there is a roadside dispute and you want to hang someone.

I look to see if he is joking, and conclude he is. Perhaps.

We are in Ivo's British-made estate car, travelling to see what some Bulgarians regard as a contender for the title of eighth wonder of the world.

Unlike most of his countrymen, Ivo drives fast but competently and with regard to other road users. He really is an exception and I still can't get used to the lunacy levels which are reflected in death and accident rates. Last year more than 700 Bulgarians were killed and more than ten thousand seriously injured. That might not sound a lot until you realise it is double the rate in the UK when you factor in the difference in population size. Interestingly in a grisly sort of way, investigation showed that 96 percent of all the deaths and accidents were the driver's fault. Ironically, the peak time for deaths is when people are going on holiday.

I have driven in most European countries, and would say that the Bulgars are the worst road users I have encountered so far. On a scale of one to ten for lunacy, I would put them at around twelve, nudging thirteen.

When I ask Ivo his opinion, he shrugs. It is just how things are, he says, and all you have to do is drive as if every other person behind the wheel you meet on a journey is blind, deaf and very stupid with a death wish. In a sober afterthought, he says that perhaps a lot of Bulgarians think they have not got much to live for.

As the weeks go by, I am beginning to understand Ivo. His default demeanour appears to be taciturn verging on sullen, but I now know there is much behind the mask, and a very acute sense of sometimes the blackest of humour. Perhaps it is just him, or perhaps it is a national trait. I don't know many Bulgarians well enough to judge, but because of the country's past I can see that what makes them smile could be of the darkest hue.

Brake lights flash, the traffic flow slows dramatically for a moment, then picks up again. I assume there has been another accident to add to the long list, but the obstruction proves to be an old van. It is moving slowly along the highway with the back doors open, and a group of men are walking solemnly behind it. They are all wearing tracksuits. As we get nearer I see the narrow end of a coffin sticking out. As we draw up behind the DIY cortege and Ivo waits to overtake, I hear a painful, squealing sound and see one of the men is holding a goat under one arm.

As I now know, the offending item is a *Gajda*. It is basically the same as the Scottish bagpipes, but the bag is made of a whole goatskin. Ivo says the pipes are sometimes played at funerals, and people say it is to make the mourners feel even more miserable. When I ask why the mourners are wearing such unsuitable clothing. He says they are not mourners. They are undertakers and the sports clothing is their uniform. It is not a Do-It-Yourself funeral, and the deceased was obviously a very tall person, which is why the casket would not fit into the hearse.

We gather speed and continue to encounter a decidedly motley collection of vehicles. Occasionally a shiny black and menacing 4 x 4 with tinted windows sweeps by, contemptuous of oncoming vehicles. Then the traffic flow slows again as we squeeze by a donkey cart, heavily laden with hay. On the back is a car registration plate which, Ivo says, is not necessary. It is just the driver's way of saying he has as much right to use the road as anyone else.

I duck instinctively as a motor bike roars into view from behind a tanker and screams towards us. Ivo does not brake but calmly pulls over a little, and the bike flashes by with the cow horn handlebars no more than a few inches from our wing mirror. The machine is a Harley Davidson, and the rider is a young man, wearing a Wild West-style leather jacket with fringes down the arms. His head is bare and his long blond hair streams out horizontally. He is wearing goggles and his eyes are wide and his face set in a manic rictus of delight. He is clearly in some sort of private world, intoxicated with the speed and the risks of driving extra-wildly in a country where road madness is the norm.

I look at Ivo, who is smiling in what looks like approval. When I ask, he says he does not know if the wearing of crash-helmets is the law, but most people do. He says this in disapproving tones, and when I ask why, he says he does not like all the health and safety rules brought in when Bulgaria joined the European Union. As another lunatic motorcyclist squeezes between us and a coach, he says it seems to him that too many people have become as scared of living as of dying.

~

After travelling for an hour northwards along a winding road through a green and pleasant land of hills and vales, we have suddenly come upon an almost alien scene.

The predominant colours are of ochre and yellow, and we could be on Mars. All around are fantastical rock formations, and two-hundred-metre fingers of time-weathered sandstone point raggedly to the sky.

The guide book says the fifty square kilometres of unearthly terrain are a by-product of the tectonic shift of two hundred million years ago that formed the Balkans, caused by erosion and even the aftermath of an inland sea.

In the way of these things, names have been given to the sometimes bizarre-looking natural sculptures, and here dwell Adam and Eve, the Lion and the Camel amongst a host of petrified legendary characters. One story tells of a ravishingly beautiful schoolgirl who was lusted after by a Dervish*. Fleeing from his attention she was confronted by a rapacious bear, and chose to be killed and eaten by it than defiled by the Dervish. But then a miracle occurred. Day became night, the earth trembled and erupted, then silence fell. When the light returned, the Schoolgirl, the Bear and the Dervish had been frozen for all eternity.

Belogradchik ('little white town') sits an hour south of the Danube and the border with Romania and in the midst of the eerie landscape. A road climbs from the town to a Roman fortress which makes the most of its dramatic surroundings.

The fort saw action in 1885 during the war between

Serbia and Bulgaria, and, along with the rocks, it is one of the few major tourist attractions in this part of the country.

Although it is the height of the season and a beautiful day, we have no problem parking and there is only a modest queue at the ticket office. It is all delightfully contra - technological as we pay for and receive our tickets from an amiable lady who records the transaction in an old ledger. There is a turnstile at the entrance, but most people simply walk round it and through an open gate alongside. Another thing I have found attractive about Bulgaria is the way that most people in authority do not seem too bothered about exerting it.

The fortress is on three levels, and I can see the now-familiar Bulgarian Health and Safety precautions are in full force. A series of steeply pitched, ancient stone stairways lead up to the top level, and some even have a handrail. I learn at the start of the climb that it is best not to rely on these rails as some of the posts supporting them are not at all securely fixed. This is great fun for the children, who enjoy frightening their mothers by pretending to stumble and teeter on the edge of the drop to the rocks below.

It is the first time I have visited a national tourist attraction and not spotted any Japanese or otherwise high-visibility foreign tourists, and the only language I hear is Bulgarian. My fellow climbers are mostly young, and very polite, some offering help on the stairs without appearing to be patronising or mocking my laboured ascent.

Ivo waits while I take a breather at each stage, and when we finally emerge at the top, the views are stunning. The little white town below fits its descriptive name exactly, and the giant rock formations rear up and stretch towards the smoky outlines of the Balkans. Any health and safety rules seem particularly ignored here, with a plethora of dodgy rails lying in wait for the unwary.

As I stand at the furthest point from any drop, a tall young man thrusts a camera at me with a smiled request, then nimbly picks his way up to the very highest point. He stands on a tiny piece of flat rock on the edge of a drop of several hundred feet and poses like a body-builder. I feel dizzy just taking the snaps. All around us, young people are outdoing each other with ever-more-risky antics for the camera, and I suggest it is time for lunch before Ivo takes on the challenge.

~

It is peak service time at what looks like a cross between a Kentucky Fried Chicken store, a kebab outlet and a fish and chip shop.

The long queue stretches outside and is surprisingly orderly. I don't know why I should find that surprising, but it could be because of the contrast with the way some Bulgarians would literally rather die than stay in their place in a moving traffic queue. It might be because I lived in France for many years, where everyone knows there is no actual word for or concept of waiting in line. Or it might just be that we Britons - and particularly we English - think we invented the queue, so lay claim to the whole ceremony and process.

The counter comes nearer, but it appears touch and go that we will reach it before every fish and chip and sausage in the shop has been taken. Then I realise that it is an ongoing process as a team of burly men emerge from off-stage to replenish and stock the hotplates.

Once again I wonder at the capacity of Bulgarians to eat more than their body weight at a sitting and appear not to pay the penalty. I am the fattest person in the queue, and could not hold a candle to some of the customers when it comes to tucking food away. The tiny lady in front of me must be half my weight and moves with picky, delicate bird-like movements as she surveys the groaning counter and selects meat balls, burgers, sausages and three types of potato. I think at first she must be ordering for her family, but all the food is piled with the skill of a seasoned *Kerplunk!* player on to one plate. The lady pays, lifts the plate with an effort, then hesitates before ordering an extra portion of chips. They are obviously to keep her going as she walks to an outside table.

Eventually we arrive at the counter and I am faced with having to make my mind up. I have been changing it on the way between steak, sausages, huge juicy burgers, kebabs, *wiener schnitzel* or the fish. And that before choosing from the half acre or so of salads and vegetable dishes.

Ivo helps make my mind up by saying we are too far from sea and river at this time of year for the mackerel or whitebait, and suggests I try the spicy chicken.

I take his advice, smile at the nearest counter hand and point at the rows of golden carcasses. The lady smiles back and rests her tongs on the counter as she looks at me expectantly. I nod and smile and point again, and Ivo sighs and says she is waiting for me to pick the actual piece I want. I do so, and as she puts it on a set of scales I realise they are selling the chicken, like the clothes in Montana, by weight. While I wait, I ask Ivo about the breaded balls in the chicken section. He breaks into a rare smile and says they are chicken's arses, not balls. I start to explain about how and why we call that bit of the bird the parson's nose, but he hustles me on to the next stage of choice.

Finally we reach the lady manning the cash register, and the bill for two plates of chicken and sausages and burgers with hot potato and other mixed salads, small mountains of coleslaw, two coffees and bottles of water and, of course, a king-size loaf comes to the equivalent of less than three pounds. Feeling guilty for no good reason, I leave a ten leva tip, but the woman at the till calls me back. Ivo explains that it does not work that way in Bulgaria. As in other civilised countries, you tip in restaurants if the service has been good, but not in takeaways.

~

On the way home, Ivo pulls off the main road and takes a winding lane which ends in the square of a small village. There is a play area, with a picnic bench, a grocery shop and a bar. Perhaps because of these facilities, the place looks somehow comfortable and at ease with itself. We drive on through and take a lane which becomes a track, at the end of which he says an English couple live. Unlike many Britons who have come to live in Bulgaria, they have become part of the community. Both are learning the language, and the wife works in a local shop while her husband works on the house.

He pulls up in a cloud of dust and sounds his horn; we get out and I do not need to be told where the English couple live.

The house is - or was - a typical communist cube, but has been redeemed and reclaimed with taste and restraint. The walls and gable end have been clad with tiles to match those on the roof, the panelled front door with its brass lion's head knocker is a brilliantly-glossed royal blue, and the hardwood sash windows fit in perfectly with the overall effect of an interesting country house of an indeterminate period. Roses actually do wind around the stable door at ground level, and beside it is what looks like an original period carriage lamp.

The gardens surrounding the house are laid to lawn and dotted with fruit trees. There is a dog kennel by the gate, and a sentry-box toilet has been surrounded with pebbles and decorated with illustrations of waves and seagulls so as to resemble what looks like a very narrow beach hut. The *piece de resistance* is a huge brick-built barbecue which is part of an open-air bar of the sort more often seen on a South Seas island resort. The owners have obviously melded all the features they liked and wanted, and it has worked very well. As I get to know the large and fortunately friendly dog, a man and a woman appear through the stable door, bearing a tray of cold drinks and snacks.

Tim and Mariah are in their fifties, and say the move to Bulgaria was so sudden they sometimes wake up and wonder at their new surroundings. They are childless by choice and in England he was a factory worker while she worked in a care home. They lived with a hefty mortgage in a two-bedroom house on a busy through-road in Loughborough, and knew they could never escape to their dream cottage in the countryside of Britain. Then they heard about the cost of property in Bulgaria and realised they could live free of debt and build the home they dreamed of in a rural setting. But the move was not just based on property prices. In the UK the couple were in dead-end jobs with the same routine every day. The challenge of going to another country, learning another language and adapting to another culture was a major spur.

A year on, and their restoration project was almost complete. The equity in their terraced house had been enough to pay for their new home and turn it into exactly what they wanted, and there was enough left for them to live on for a year or so. The next challenge would be to set up a small business offering building and other services to Britons with homes in the province. If that did not work, they would do something else. They had no fear for the future as they had proved what they could do together. The neighbours could not be nicer or the villagers more friendly, and Fred the mastiff was in dog Heaven.

We drove off as they stood in the garden waving; they were holding hands and I do not think it was for show.

They are a perfect example of the sort of expatriates who are happy to be in a foreign land because they are happy to be together. From what I know and have seen, they are in the minority.

There is no practical way of finding out how many Britons own a holiday home or live in Bulgaria, but the latest estimate is around 18,000. Many have bought a home or moved to live here simply because of the ultra-low cost of living and the almost risible price of property. As so many British expats have found out to their cost in financial and emotional terms, this is not a good basis on which to make a life-changing move. If price and a sunny climate were to be the only consideration for a going to live in a foreign country, there would be thriving British expat communities in downtown Mogadishu or a slum *favela* in Brasilia.

I have met and heard from hundreds of Britons who have moved abroad to live but have come back wiser and poorer. The saddest are those who cannot afford to go home, which makes their enforced residency in a foreign land even more painful. But it works to all sorts of levels and degrees for hundreds of thousands.

In his satirical work *The Devil's Dictionary*, 19th-century author Ambrose Bierce defined immigrants as 'unenlightened people who think one country is better than another'.

I take his point, and, whatever they say, some people who move to live in a new land are trying to escape from themselves. But it does suit many to make a new life in a new land, and it seems to me that Bulgaria is a good place to start a life anew.

*Arriving in Bulgaria as part of the colonisation process by the Ottoman Empire, 'Whirling Dervishes' spin as an aid to meditation. You may have seen the men in hugely wide skirts rotating hypnotically in television advertisements promoting Turkey as a holiday destination.

Though they don't use aubergines in their version of *moussaka*, Bulgars like this easy-to-make spread which is often used in a salad:

Кьопоолу
Kyopoolu
(aubergine salad/spread)

Ingredients

Three aubergines
Four red bell peppers
Four cloves of garlic
Some fresh parsley
Two tablespoons of red wine vinegar
Some olive oil
Some seasoning

Method

1. Poke holes in the aubergines
2. Roast them and the peppers in an oven set to 180°C for about forty minutes
3. When skins blister, take out of oven and cover and leave for ten minutes
4. Peel the aubergines and peppers and chop into small pieces after de-seeding
5. Season and add a splash of vinegar
6. Crush the garlic and add to the mix
7. Top with the parsley and drizzle oil over

This is another dish enjoyed by several countries in the Balkans region, though surprisingly, the Greeks and Arabic nations give each other the credit with this one. To the Greeks it is *moussaka*, and they believe it was invented when Arabs brought the aubergine to their country. Its ancestor can certainly be found in a 13th-century collection of recipes known as the Baghdad Cookbook. Arabs think of the dish as Greek or Turkish, and The Bulgarian version uses potatoes instead of aubergine and does not include courgettes:

Мусака
Musaka
(Moussaka)

Ingredients

5 tablespoons of olive oil
500g minced beef
1 teaspoon paprika
1 teaspoon cumin
1 teaspoon salt
1 teaspoon pepper
Four potatoes, peeled and made into small cubes
A tin of pulped tomatoes
One beaten egg
A cup of yogurt

Method

1. Preheat the oven to 165°C
2. Fry the beef mince in the oil until evenly brown
3. Season and add spices, stir in potatoes and cook for another three minutes or so
4. Stir in the tomatoes

5. Add a little water and reduce heat and simmer for fifteen minutes
6. Put the mixture in a baking dish
7. Mix the egg and yogurt and pour over
8. Bake for half an hour or so or until top is golden brown

Nobody would claim crème caramel as having a Bulgarian origin, but it is immensely popular and likely to appear on the menu of most restaurants. This is one of the ways they like it made:

крем карамел
tsreme karamel
(crème caramel)

Ingredients

A litre of warm milk
Eight eggs
Half a cup of sugar
One teaspoon vanilla extract
A pinch of cinnamon
10 suitable small oven-proof containers

Method

1. Mix the eggs and milk well and stir in half the sugar
2. Add the vanilla and cinnamon
3. Test and add more sugar to taste
4. Melt the rest of the sugar in a non-stick pan and do not let it burn
5. Add some water to make the melting easier
6. Pour the melted sugar into the cups, ensuring you cover the bottoms
7. Add the egg and milk mix
8. Place cups in cold water so that water level reaches the same height as the level of the mixture in the cups
9. Bake for 25 minutes until a golden-brown crust is formed on top
10. Turn out on to plates

Треска за злато
Gold fever

Summer is on the wing, and soon the birds of passage will be off in search of warmer climes. I too will be leaving, and with much regret. But for now the sun shines brightly, and there is enough blue in the vast dome above the valley to make an army of Dutchmen's trousers*.

Another excursion with Ivo today, and we are going in search of gold and ancient treasures.

Before that, I must pay the daily bribe to Muttley and his mates, take breakfast beneath a convenient fruit tree, then pay a visit to the village cemetery with Ivalin. He says it is at the bottom of the valley, and the final few hundred metres are so steep and treacherous that visitors and even the deceased have to leave their vehicles at the top of the slope. We, of course, will be driving right to the gates. I replied that I just hoped we would be coming back.

~

Ivalin was not exaggerating. I suppose the cemetery was

built so far away from the village to prevent contagion, and perhaps at the bottom of such a hard climb to dissuade ghouls and ghosts from making the return trip.

As I climb into the van and brace myself for what is to come, I ask Ivalin if Bulgarians are superstitious, and he looks at me as if to see if it is a serious question.

His countrymen, he said, have a lot to be superstitious about. It is a known fact that, like so many dishes and drinks and customs claimed by other countries, vampirism actually originated in Bulgaria. For evidence, he cited a recent and gruesome discovery in two medieval graves near a monastery in the Black Sea town of Sozopol. The bodies in the graves both had iron rods driven through where their hearts would have been. It was a not uncommon practice right up until the beginning of the last century, and, contrary to myth, was not done to kill vampires. It was to pin them in their coffins to stop them terrorising the locality.

Bulgaria (naturally) had its own type of vampires, called *ustrels*. This creature was a child born on a Saturday who died before being baptised. The ustrel would leave its grave to feed on the blood of cattle and sheep, and hide during the day between the horns of a ram or the back legs of a milk cow. When I told him about the man we saw lying under a cow and examining its teats he said it was possible he was looking for an ustrel but, more likely and as Richard had suggested, a free drink.

~

I now know why the cemetery lies so far from the village.

Ivalin says there is a story that, long ago, a number of Turkish occupiers were killed by local men and buried here. One of the Turks' dogs escaped, led an army unit to the spot and nearby Krasiva was burned to the ground in reprisal. The 'new' village developed at the top of the hill over the centuries.

If true, I suppose it gives more impetus to Sally Moore's drive to save Krasiva. How sad that a village put to death and then returning phoenix-like from the ashes should die again from simple circumstance.

~

Even in busy cities, cemeteries seem to have a sense of stillness. In this isolated and remote place, it is literally as quiet as the grave. The rasp and creak of the wrought-iron gates opening is magnified by the utter silence. The nearest road is through the village a mile up the track, and donkey carts do not make much noise. Even the birds seem to avoid this lonely spot.

I am used to rural France, where cemeteries are kept completely pristine by relatives, so to me this one looks rather forlorn. It is overgrown with long grass and weed, one of the walls is crumbling and there is a general air of neglect. Walking to the well-kept family plot where his parents and grandparents rest, Ivalin says the problem is that most of the people buried here have no living relatives, their families have moved away, or their survivors are too old or infirm to make the journey. There has only been one funeral here in recent years, and that was just last week. He points to a corner plot, and the mystery of the marble slabs standing against a wall in the Mud House is solved. They were not for renovation or improvement work, but to be used as headstones for the elderly couple who died within weeks of each other.

I leave Ivalin with his family for a moment, then as we walk back to the van he tells me about rural funeral traditions and customs. In Bulgaria, he says, many people believe that our fate and fortunes are determined at birth, but Death always comes unannounced. When it happens, windows are opened, plates turned upside down and mirrors and pictures are covered. Money may be put in the pockets of the deceased so he or she can buy themselves a better life in the hereafter. Eyes are always closed as failure to do so may pre-empt another imminent death.

We bucket and bounce at the usual lunatic pace up the track and back towards the village, and I ask Ivalin if he believes in predestination and a pre-set appointment with Death. He is silent for a moment, probably thinking of his mother, then says many people in Bulgaria believe in fate. It may be a comfort to some, or an excuse to do nothing to make life better. He has changed his life by his own efforts, but most of the people in the cemetery would have thought that when and how they would arrive there was beyond their control.

~

There is something decidedly bloke-ish about hobby conventions and celebrations, and this one is no exception.

The way to the event is indicated by the effigy of a giant prospector with a spade-like beard and fur hat. He is dressed in a suitable checked shirt and bib and brace overalls, and his pickaxe points to a path through fields to where the event is taking place. An interesting collection of mostly battered cars, vans and pick-up trucks lines the main road, some left as if in direct challenge to passing traffic. The all-male stream of enthusiasts flows along the path, and its constituents are as distinct and singular in their appearance as their vehicles.

An interest in or lust for gold knows no boundaries, so the enthusiasts come in all styles, ages and sizes. In front of us is a group of no-necks, all wearing black tee-shirts which look as if they are restraining a writhing bunch of eels. Walking beside them is a group of what looks like New Age travellers or former members of Dexie's Midnight Runners; one of their number is stripped to the waist but protecting his head with a cap made from a giant dock leaf. It looks as if there may be a Most Eccentric Headwear event as part of the activities, and there is a profusion of cowboy hats, ball caps, straw Panamas and even Mexican sombreros. Given that the owners spend long hours under the blazing sun while searching for gold, they are a sensible choice, but I can't see the purpose of the World War II aviator's cap (goggles included), or the stovepipe hat with the top detached and sticking up like the lid of a half-opened tin can.

At the end of the track is another lofty figure, assumedly giving us further directions. This one is a little shorter and a lot slenderer than the prospector, and is wearing an Indiana Jones hat and a long white goatee beard which puts me in mind of the eponymous hero of the 1970's television series about a time travelling wizard, *Catweasel*. As we get closer, the effigy moves, and Ivo introduces me to one of the organisers of the event.

Our host is an obviously learned man and interested in gold for more than its monetary value. He speaks good but heavily accented English which makes his story more evocative as he talks of Bulgaria as the cradle of the Thracian civilisation, and a race famed for crafting exquisite jewellery from the gold in which the country is naturally rich. Panning for gold has been legal since 2009, and no licence is required. Those who strike it lucky are required to pay ten percent of the value of their find in tax. The government claims that nearly all rivers are gold-bearing but he thinks they are wrong. But some people do make a living from working every day for long hours in secret places. River gold is usually of a relatively low quality of around 20 carats, and the banks will pay around fifty leva (£20) per gram. He adds that Bulgaria is a poor country, so any way of making a little extra money is bound to be popular. Unlike many unofficial activities, river panning is at least legal.

As we walk away, Ivo says that what our host didn't say was that many of the enthusiasts here go in for gold prospecting in a big way, and some are professionals. Plastic panning dishes are for those who play at it. Also, many people here will not restrict their gold hunting to rivers, but use metal detectors to find ancient buried treasure. He does not say so, but I know Ivo is a keen detectorist.

We reach the site of the event, which is alongside several hundred metres of riverbank. A field has been mown and marked out with posts and pennants, and along one side is a line of square, tall tents with metal machinery glinting in the sun. Even at this distance, I can hear the jumble of amplified music and commercial announcements, with salesmen's pitches competing with the skirl of bagpipes and Western pop. With the hubbub and colourful flags and tall square tents, it has the air of a modern-day jousting contest, but the competition here will be for finding hidden gold.

We follow the course of the river, which is swift-flowing and shallow, with the bed covered with shingle and stones up to a foot across. Small, almost transparent fish weave unconcernedly in and out of the larger rocks. Perhaps they know that the men lining the bank are fishing only for gold.

The bank is lined with tents and accommodations of all types. There are single-occupier pup tents, traditional ridge tents and some very grand affairs. One has a pergola-type awning outside, beneath which a middle-aged man is working on a barbecue. In the open air, the smell of cooking is intoxicating.

Away from the encampment, a couple of men with their trousers rolled to their knees are crouching by a kink in the river where the water swirls round and then moves slowly on. I had hoped that the panners would be using old-fashioned, dented tin dishes as in prospecting movies, but they are actually wielding brightly coloured plastic discs which look like those you see children throwing for dogs in parks.

There is a cough, splutter and then a roar nearby, and we turn to where a couple of young men are bending over a strange-looking device. It is a square red box on legs, and from it protrudes a flat metal runnel with raised sides. On the floor of the runnel is a grid, and beneath that what looks like a piece of carpeting. From the back of the other side of the box a wide flexible tube disappears into the river. Alongside the box is the generator we heard firing up.

One of the men stands up, and his lean, tallness is emphasised by the wet suit he is wearing. He and Ivo exchange a volley of what is obviously familiar banter, then the man laughs and steps into the river and sits down up to his waist. Ivo explains that the two prospectors are partners and had tossed a coin to see who would look after the machine and who would sit in the river. In the winter the lucky one gets to stay on the shore, but on a day like today it is a good job to be the one in the water.

The man in the river grabs the handles on the end of the tube and thrusts it down towards the bed. Immediately, there is a heavy clattering as stones are sucked into the tube and propelled into the square box. The man on the bank begins sorting out the larger ones, throwing them back into the river while he allows the pebble-sized ones to pass through the box and then along the runnel. From there the debris falls off the end and into the water. As he moves the tube around and gathers more and more material, the man in the river settles lower and Ivo says he will be up to his neck before long. Then they will find another spot.

We walk over to the box and Ivo explains that any fragments falling through the grid will be trapped in the carpet of felt-like material. I ask if they will make much money today, and Ivo shrugs and speaks to the man on the bank. He apes the shrug, then takes something from his pocket and hands it to me. It is a small, plastic tube with a stopper, and something is glittering inside it. I hold it up to eye level and see a dozen or so small, misshapen lumps. They have a dull sheen, and look like a gold tooth filling that fell out when I bit too hard on a nut one Christmas. I look impressed and mime my congratulations and ask Ivo how much the haul is worth and if they found it today. He smiles grimly and says the value would be no more than two hundred Euros. He does not know how long it would have taken them to collect it, but probably weeks. Prospectors bring their stashes to show off at events like this, and some even buy nuggets to make it look as if they have been more successful than others. The machine would have cost about three hundred Euros, and would take a while to pay for. But it was more than money that the men were here for.

I use up a hefty slice of my Bulgarian vocabulary to wish the machine men good luck, and we move upriver to where the couple are panning with their Frisbees.

As we arrive, they both get to their feet and say hello, observing protocol by shaking my hand first. There is another exchange as Ivo obviously asks if they are having any luck, and the Bulgarian shrug comes into play. I have become something of an expert on classifying all degrees and varieties of national European shrugs and what they mean. The standard British shrug in response to any query usually means 'Dunno, mate, you'd better ask someone else.' The frustrated Italian shrug expresses astonishment at how cruel/stupid/ insensitive the rest of the world can be, and the default French shrug states 'Frankly, I don't give a shit about you and your problems.' It is early days, but it seems to me that the standard Bulgarian shrug is almost Arabic in implication, as if the user is demonstrating acceptance of the world and what it has dealt out to him. But the version these gold seekers have been using is more of an 'if you like' gesture.

The taller and older of the two reaches into the breast pocket of his overalls and pulls out a small envelope. He opens it carefully and even more carefully shakes a few specks into the palm of his hand. He prods one with a finger and says something, and Ivo translates. The gold is not from today, but yesterday. They came a day earlier to steal a march on the other prospectors, but found there were already a dozen tents on the bank belonging to people with the same idea. If I used their magnifying glass I would see that the specks of gold they found late last night had quite sharp edges. This is very good news, as the further the nuggets travel from the vein, the more worn they become. He would ask us not to tell anyone else, but their plan was to seek sharper and sharper specks to indicate the proximity of the vein. That's if they found any, of course. Mostly, the trick was spotting the gold amongst all the crap.

He sees me looking at his Frisbee, smiles and asks through Ivo if I would like a go. I nod eagerly and he hands over the panning dish and shows me where to kneel. Ivo says he says that gold is twenty times heavier than water and moves slower and may gather where there are obstructions. The best place to pan is in the gravel by tree roots or under large stones at bends in the river.

I take the pan and follow his instructions and slosh some gravelly water into the dish. Then I swirl it round and gradually let the water dribble over the edge so that the sand and smaller gravel remains. Something is glittering in the coating at the bottom of the pan, and I excitedly shout that I have had beginner's luck. The man takes the pan and looks closely at the bottom, then gives it another swirl before rinsing it in the water.

As Ivo tells me they say in gold-hunting circles, all that

glitters in a pan is definitely not gold. Everyone has heard of fool's gold, which is called pyrite. It is as beautiful as gold but has little value. The shiny flakes I had brought up were the mineral mica. The going rate is about ten Euros a tonne. Gold is of course so valuable because it is so rare. If you find half a gram from every cubic metre of gravel you shift, you are doing well. To get an idea of what hard work it is, a cubic metre of gravel means about a hundred bucketfuls of gravel to be sifted through. That is of course many thousands of pans-worth.

~

We may be sixteen hundred miles away from my local County Show, but the sound of badly positioned loudspeakers and microphones is familiar to anyone who has attended this sort of an outdoor event. The humming and squealing is followed by the inevitable and hugely amplified tap of a forefinger against the microphone.

Then comes the gale-like blowing into it as if a giant were cooling his tea. Finally comes what even I can translate as someone saying 'ONE, ONE, ONE' in the robotic monotone which is *de rigueur* for microphone testing.

Ivo says that this is a sign The Blessing is about to take place, and, full of curiosity I follow him towards the source of the noise.

We find the sound system set up in front of what must be the organisers' tent, and a small man in a ball cap, tee-shirt, jeans and trainers is standing on tiptoe to use the microphone. He has some prepared notes and starts with what is obviously a welcome to all attendees. Listening to speeches is, for me, one of the fun parts of being at a function in a country where I know little of the language. The game is to guess what the speaker is saying, and see if you are proved right by what happens next. In this case I am not even close, and the man is now pointing at a row of metal detectors lined up on the grass in front of him.

As he speaks, a burly man cocks a leg over the string of pennants and adds a detector to the row. The speaker gives him a look of admonition, clears his throat, and starts again.

I can see that he is working his way up to the climax of his address, and reaching it, he twirls away from the microphone and, like a compere introducing a star turn, extends an arm in the direction of the tent.

I do not know what or who I expected to emerge from the tent, but it was certainly not a priest in full ecclesiastical fig.

An estimated eighty percent of Bulgarians are Christian, and the Bulgarian Orthodox Church claims another two million worldwide. It is one of the oldest church movements in the world, and was officially recognised in 927 AD. In administrative terms, Bulgaria is divided into thirteen dioceses, which are sub-divided into parishes. There are 1,500 priests ministering to those parishes.

I don't know what the salary is, but this priest could earn a fortune playing one in soaps and films. He is at least a foot taller than the man who introduced him, and the dramatic effect of his appearance is enhanced by his ecclesiastical garb.

His high-collared, wide-sleeved black cassock reaches to the ground, and a narrow white embroidered stole is draped around his shoulders and falls to below his knees.

His carefully-coiffed hair is as black as his robe and he has a very neatly trimmed and narrow beard following his firm jaw line. By any standards, he is extremely handsome, with what looks like a natural tan, small neat features, the straightest of noses and, even seen from this distance, large eyes looking beyond his immediate surroundings. In his hands he holds a weighty and time-worn book. In any horror flick he would be a shoo-in for the priest who tries to exorcise Dracula and ends up as his victim. In real life, wherever he has his living I bet he stirs the hearts of more than a few female parishioners and nuns, and even perhaps a few monks.

He walks with shoulders back and head erect towards the microphone, and there is a moment's awkwardness while the compere struggles to adjust the stand so the priest does not have to bend down to use it. Finally, all is ready. I notice that a crowd has gathered. Most are still wearing their eccentric headgear, but are respectfully attentive.

Then, just as the priest opens his mouth there is a huge burst of noise. It is the refrain from the 1960s pop classic, *The Night has a Thousand Eyes* by Bobby Vee and I note it is the original version. The thunderous noise comes from the Bulgarian equivalent of a burger van parked nearby, but stops within seconds. Somehow it enhances the dramatic effect as the priest begins his routine. He has a deep and powerful voice which ranges through the octaves. To me it sounds like a cross between the yodelling chants heard at a High Church Mass and the wailing from a minaret as the muezzin calls the faithful to prayer.

That part of the ceremony over, the priest closes his book, picks up what looks like a shaving bowl with an oversized brush and walks along the line of metal detectors. It makes for a surreal scene as he shakes holy water on to the machines while speaking with a dirge-like intonation.

He reaches the end of the line and returns to his position by the microphone as the owners retrieve their metal detectors. I assume the ceremony is over, but it seems the priest is reluctant to waste the holy water or the opportunity. The little man in the ball cap stands on his toes and speaks into the microphone, and several men detach themselves from the audience and step over the ropes. They are joined by others, and soon there is a queue standing in front of the celebrant. This time, hats are doffed as the queue shuffles forward. Ivo and I look at each other, then he shrugs and we step over the rope.

It is the first time I have been anointed with holy water and I am unsure whether I should thank the priest or make any sort of gesture. In the end, I lift a hand and self-consciously start to make the sign of the Cross as the water hits me in the face. The priest's eyes narrow, so for fear of offending or doing his job for him, I turn the sign into a little wave of the type one makes when saying a tentative goodbye to someone you do not know well. He looks even more bemused and gives me an extra spray of holy water as if he thinks I may need it.

~

Another thing I like about this country is that so many Bulgarian dishes seem to have been created with eating outdoors in mind. The unpretentious food smells and tastes so good in the open air, and a lot of it can be eaten between slices of bread. This could explain why there are so many kebab shops in every European country.

It is not yet noon, but a longer queue is lining up to eat than received the blessing.

At these sort and size of events in Britain, there would normally be a franchise awarded to one or two burger vans. Here there are three in a row, and all are doing good business. Rather than serving from their vans, the owners and their helpers stand behind a long row of tables. Some are bowed beneath the weight of platters of burgers and sausages, chicken wings and breasts and meat balls. There are also bowls of salad and mountains of chips, and of course heaps of domed white loaves. Each table also has a beer pump fixed to it. It is all very convivial as the customers move along the tables, making their choices and paying and then continuing to the undercover dining area. There is even a music-while-you-wait system, with the caterers presenting a medley of interestingly clashing tunes. A selection of bagpipe music is issuing from the loudspeaker on the roof of one van, while next door Bobby Vee is being aired again. Alongside them, the owner of the third van is looking smug. He has the biggest loudspeaker, and it is belting out a very suitable rendition of *Gold Fever* from the musical *Paint Your Wagon*.

The line moves on and I collect my kyufte meatball/burger, two spicy sausages, a skip of cheesy chips and then add some lettuce leaves and a tomato for healthy eating reasons. Ivo chooses a more modest selection, and I pay the bill. With large glasses of beer and a couple of bottles of water, it comes to about the cost of a cup of skinny *latte* in a snobby we-saw-you-coming London café.

The undercover area is busy, but we have been saved places on the bench seating at a long table reserved for club officials and their friends. They look like interesting dinner companions.

At one end is Catweasel, his goatee bobbing as he eats and talks. Alongside him is a man who makes the gypsy king of Krasiva look almost diminutive. Ivo says the giant is an old friend and his nickname is Panther. Ivo pronounces the name as 'Panzer' and it suits, as his pal looks as intimidating and powerful as a tank. Like his neighbour, Panther wears a goatee, but it is coal-black and thicker and more restrained. He is otherwise clean shaven, including his head, and wears a large gold earring. With his olive skin, dark eyes and full lips he looks as if he should be guarding the entrance to a harem, his great meaty hands resting on the hilt of a giant scimitar. He is also wearing a thick, rope-styled gold chain around his neck that looks as if it would take several years worth of non-stop panning to supply the raw material. Beneath the chain I can see a livid scar which runs around his throat. When I ask Ivo about it, he says that Panther was a doorman at a night club some years ago and threw a troublesome customer out. The man was local, and returned with some friends and a knife. When I ask what happened to the attacker, Ivo gives an unconcerned Bulgarian shrug, then says nobody knows as he disappeared shortly after the fracas. I look at the size of Panther's forearms and wonder how long it would take him to dig a man-sized hole with his prospecting tools.

Sitting opposite us is an entirely different character. He is of middle age, slight and wearing a two-piece suit which has obviously become an old friend. A pair of rimless spectacles held together with sticky tape sit on top of his head. Overall, he has the air of someone more interested in things other than his appearance. Ivo introduces him as Lubo, a very clever man who makes and sells metal detectors. He could be a millionaire, says Ivo in respectful tones, but refuses to become a friend and slave of money.

We shake hands and Lubo raises an eyebrow and toasts me with his near-empty beer glass, then drains it and returns it to the table as if having made a significant effort. He is clearly so laid-back he is at risk of falling off the bench, and his mildly amused expression is of a man who understands life and what a bad joke it can be.

I offer him a beer which he graciously accepts, and he offers me a cigarette which I regretfully refuse.

When I return, Lubo is holding a conversation with a large green lizard. It quite casually climbs down his trouser leg and goes to investigate the next table as I deliver our beers. We clink glasses and he asks what I am doing here and gives a lazy smile when I tell him. He asks if it is true that only poor Britons are moving to live in Bulgaria, and when I say I don't know, he says he hopes so. The world, he continues, has gone mad for money, which is why so many of his countrymen and women are leaving Bulgaria. True Bulgarians know that there is more to life than a new car, but the younger generation has not been taught that simple truth. It is a shame, he says, as it means his country will end up filled with old people. There is nothing wrong in being old, he adds, but there is no future for a country which is deserted by its children.

~

I have been to this village before, and the gaunt Soviet-era square is normally sparsely occupied and depressingly drab. But today it is full of people, life, colour and sound.

In France, they have fêtes and saints to celebrate all sorts of food and drink. I know of a *fête de la carrotte* in Normandy where you can eat carrot cake and bread, drink carrot wine and even play chess with pieces made from carrots. Today, we are here to pay tribute to the watermelon.

On the way back from the gold rush we left the highway, negotiated a road block and came to this small town to join hundreds of people for the festivities.

There are many events like this across Bulgaria, and some draw huge crowds. There is a two-day festival at Salmanovo in the north-east which attracts six thousand visitors, some from far-away countries.

This is a more modest affair, but we are promised blindfold melon eating and throwing contests, a prize for the biggest specimen, and even a watermelon fight. There will also be a competition for the best decorated and carved watermelon sculptures. There will certainly be no shortage of raw materials, as the official production figure nationwide is 68 thousand tons. This works out to something like ten watermelons for every woman, man and infant in the country.

To those in the know, watermelon is often described as a

vegetable disguised as a fruit, though is technically a berry and very ancient in origin. Watermelon seeds were found in the tomb of Tutankhamun. Size seems to know no limits, and the largest recorded watermelon was grown in Tennessee in 2013 and weighed in at 159 kilos.

Today's event is simply to celebrate the end of the season as an excuse to have some fun and use up a surplus of richness. The price plummets from around 49 stotinki (less than twenty pence) a kilo at the beginning of August, and today they are giving it away.

Lining the square are stalls serving free slices of melon and paid-for food and drink, and a stage at the end of the square offers displays of traditional dancing and even a troupe of acrobats. As we arrive, a squadron of bagpipers is warming up, competing with a dozen sources of amplified music. It is all splendidly chaotic, and makes for the infectious air of jollity of a travelling fair.

We pause to take part in a guess-the-weight-of-the-watermelon competition and watch the judging for the best-looking specimen. They look identical to me, but the individual merits and flaws are being as fiercely debated as at any fruit and vegetable competition in a village fete in England.

We pass a stall where several people are wearing blindfolds and being fed watermelon. I don't know what the objective or rules are, but everyone is having a good time. A hugely fat man is popping the buttons on his shirt as he strains forward to gorge on the slice held by his partner, a dainty-looking little woman.

We sidestep the 'who-can-spit-the-watermelon-seed-the-furthest' contest and stop where a small crowd has gathered to watch a woman carving watermelons into floral displays. It is quite breathtakingly skilful, but she makes it look easy to turn a solid lump of pulp and flesh into the most delicate of creations. The melon she is working on is becoming a whole basket of fruits, each sculpted to suit the varying shades and colour of the flesh.

There are red cherries and pale lemons and even oranges which look good enough to eat, and obviously are. It would be offensive to do so, and there is something poignant about the way that something so hard-won, delicate and beautiful will rot and die in days.

Even though we ate so well at the gold rush, the aroma of food cooking in the open air is irresistible, and we queue up to buy *kebapche* and chips. Apart from minor recipe differentials, this striped fish finger-sized and shaped delicacy is a *kofte* by any other name and tastes just as good.

Another bout of howl-round, giant's finger-tapping and tea-cooling and Ivo tells me the man at the microphone is saying the dancing is about to start. Not, he adds, dancing for us, but a display of traditional Bulgarian *kitka* dancing. I follow him and we join the crowd moving towards the stage as a group of colourfully dressed women appear on it.

The five performers who form a line vary in age from teens to extreme maturity, and are dressed identically. They wear flower garlands in their hair and heavily embroidered black and white shift-type dresses which reach below the knees. Their slim waists are emphasised by belts made from lengths of material with bobbles at the ends. The outfits are completed with red stockings and sandal-style shoes.

At a signal from off-stage, the troupe links up by crossing arms and holding hands at waist level with their next-but-one neighbour by gripping each side of a lacy handkerchief.

A slight pause, then the pretty lady at the end gives a slight nod, and we are off.

The music blasts out from the loudspeakers, which, along with the actions of the ladies, reminds me of a western line dance. There is a rhythmic pounding beat marking time for what sounds like an accordion or an organ set to sound like a fiddle.

There is a ripple of applause as the line moves back and forward and to each side, the dancers high-stepping and performing intricate cross-overs. It is all effortless and decidedly joyful. Next the line breaks and the dancers turn and twist in unison, one hand on hip, the other aloft and twirling a handkerchief. The pace becomes ever faster, but still they make it look effortless as they part and meet and kick and hop.

Suddenly, everything stops and the mood changes dramatically. The jolly plonking is replaced by a soulful wailing and the movements on stage are slow and reflective. I do not need to understand the words to know they talk of the reality of the often hardships of life and lost love in the countryside. But then, the music and the mood changes as the pace picks up and the dancers take on and defeat the sombre ambience. Faster and faster they move, sometimes seeming to deliberately outpace the music. Finally, a great crescendo and they freeze and all is silent for a split second before a thunderous applause washes across the square.

Ivo and I look at each other and I think he knows that I know what the dance and the music says about life through the ages in a country with such a long history of oppression and adversity.

~

We are on the way home, and I am thinking about the mood at the festival today. People were out to enjoy themselves and clearly did. There was no drunkenness or anti-social behaviour that I saw, just a lot of ordinary people having a fun day out.

In my short time here it seems to me that people are certainly no more unhappy than elsewhere I have travelled in Europe. Yet, if a survey is to be believed, Bulgarians consider themselves the unhappiest people in

Europe. A survey on the ridiculously-named International Day of Happiness claimed Bulgaria scored only 4.8 on a scale of 0-10, some way behind the next most miserable European country which was Portugal with 6.2. Top of the ratings were the Scandinavians, who scored eight out of ten. It is true that Bulgaria is one of the poorest countries in Europe and the Scandinavian countries are amongst the richest, but I do not think it can be as simple as that. I ask Ivo for his opinion, and he smiles for at least the second time in the day. It is a grim smile, but still a smile.

To begin with, he says, the survey was obviously bullshit. But the real reason his countrymen and women scored so low was that they judge happiness differently.

To begin with Bulgarians are superstitious and would not claim to be happy in case it challenged the fates. Also, Bulgarians know too much to be empty-headedly happy. As the Bible says, with much wisdom comes much sorrow. Finally, Bulgarians are honest. In the rest of Europe, it is almost as bad to admit to not being manically happy all the time, to confess to wanting to have sex with children. Quite simply, the other countries lied more than the Bulgarians when they answered the questions.

We drive on in reflective silence for a few moments, then he looks at me and gives that grim smile again, and says that any impartial observer with a knowledge of history would admit that his people have a lot more to be unhappy about than many other European countries. Or perhaps it is simply that his people are so poor they *think* they should be unhappy...

This traditional Bulgarian starter or snack reminds me of the sort of cheese and pineapple-on-a-stick tit-bits we used to dish up at student parties. Although it is so seemingly obvious, I bet few people elsewhere have tried this combo:

диня и бяло сирене
dinya i byalo sirene
(watermelon with white cheese)

Ingredients

500g chilled watermelon
250g sirene (feta-style cheese)
Some lime juice
Some mint leaves

Method

1. Peel and de-seed the watermelon
2. Cut into bite-sized cubes
3. Cut the cheese into similar-sized chunks
4. Squeeze lime juice over cubes and adorn with mint leaves

We tried this potato casserole as a side dish at the gold rush event. Local cooks like to add onion slices but that is not a countrywide tradition:

Българските сирене картофи
Bulgarskite sirene kartofi
(Cheesy Bulgarian potatoes)

Ingredients

Six large potatoes cut in very thin slices
100g butter
Two large onions
500g feta-style cheese
Two eggs
250ml plain yogurt

Method

1. Mix the cheese with the softened butter and some seasoning
2. Put a layer of the potato slices in a greased baking tray
3. Lay some thinly sliced onion over the potato slices
4. Spread some yogurt and the cheese and butter mix over
5. Repeat the process
6. Cover the top with a mix of the yogurt and beaten eggs
7. Put a lid or foil over the top
8. Cook in an oven at 190°C for an hour or so, removing the foil/lid for the last ten minutes

This is another variety of banitsa, this time featuring pumpkin. It is traditionally served on Christmas Eve:

Тиквеник
Tikvenik
(pumpkin and walnuts in filo pastry)

Ingredients

400g ready-made filo pastry
350g grated pumpkin
A cup of coarsely chopped walnuts
Half a cup caster sugar
Some vegetable oil
Two teaspoons of cinnamon
Some dusting sugar

Method

1. Preheat your oven to 180°C
2. Grease the bottom of a baking pan
3. Mix the pumpkin, walnuts, cinnamon and sugar in a bowl
4. Put a tablespoon of the mix at one end of a filo sheet
5. Roll the sheet over the mixture and place in the baking pan with a little oil on top
6. Repeat the process
7. Bake for around twenty minutes or until your rolls are golden brown
8. Dust with the powdered sugar before serving

години магарешки
Donkey's years

Some houses steal your heart on sight and you can't say why. This one steals mine because it fulfils all my long held fantasies of what comprises the ideal rural retreat.

To start with, the nearest neighbour is out of sight but only a hundred yards away, so the property is alone but not isolated.

Unusually, it stands away from the gate in the middle of an acre or so. Quite sensibly, our ancestors preferred their homes to be as close as possible to a dry track. The gardens and grounds surrounding the house are flat, but it stands half-way up the hill and so has panoramic views across the valley and to the mountain ranges beyond.

On top of all that, it is one of the old-style village houses and has been renovated with style, sympathy and flair. The outside walls are snow white, criss-crossed with beams rough-crafted from mountain chestnut. Hand-carved wooden finials and other architectural decorations enhance the gable end, and a walkway and balcony runs along the upper floor. From there, the sunsets will be more than spectacular.

There is much more about this ideal home to salivate

over, but from my wife's point of view its most attractive feature is that it is not for sale.

The reason I cannot buy this wonderful old house on the spot is not only because its value would exceed the limit on my credit card, but because it belongs to one of Sally and Richard's first recruits to the Krasiva arts and crafts commune. The owner lives in France, where she makes designer handbags. She is also a very talented musician, providing me with another reason to resent her. My hosts have brought me here to see what can be done with a lot of imaginative thinking and a very small amount of money by western European standards.

Another selling point for me is that the cottage sits on a foundation of stone blocks which may have been shaped and dressed two thousand years ago. As Richard explains, the upper structures of this type of home were timber frames, infilled with unfired home-made bricks. But for strength of support, the basements were made with very solid blocks of stone. The ones used in this house look as if they may have come from the remains of the Roman fort at the top of the track.

Another attractive and unusual feature is that the roof has been stripped, new joists fitted and the original and distinctive half-round tawny-hued roof tiles put back. They are a reminder of the distant past and still known as Turkish tiles. A simple but clever design feature is that they overhang the walls by several feet. This was done to protect the unbaked bricks from rain, and the process made guttering unnecessary.

Inside, the plain and simple artfulness of the layout makes me even more resentful. The bedrooms are downstairs, and the whole of the first floor has been given over to an open-plan living space. Dark oak beams and flooring contrast with the stark white rough rendering, and the wooden furniture is solid and simple in the style favoured by the Arts and Crafts movement.

Down to the rich, meaty smell of the wood-stain, it is all

just so perfect and exactly how I would have done it had I the taste. For me, it examples the ideal blend of a feel of a past that never was and, yet the modern kitchen and bathroom blend happily in with the whole. Having tried the simple life in leaky cabins and mostly ruined farm buildings in rural France, I have no desire to get away from it all and live without the luxuries we now regard as essentials. There is electricity here, and a genuine Aga, and a power shower and a flushing toilet, so it is not at all representative of the past. But it would be easy to sit here on a winter's night with the lights off and stove roaring and think yourself back two centuries and more.

~

We have walked up the track to the nearest neighbouring property.

It too is an ancient cottage in its own grounds, but unlike the one we have just inspected it has clearly never been renovated, just patchily repaired. One corner of the roof is covered by a large tarpaulin, and the much-mended walls are a variety of colours. In contrast, the front door and windows are new and made of white plastic.

There is an old shed alongside the house, and next to it a sentry box toilet is threatened by a monstrous pile of sawn logs and branches. A handful of hens scratch around a compost heap near their run, watched over by a magnificently arrogant cock.

Apart from a pathway leading from the gate to the front door, virtually every other inch of the half-acre gardens is in use to produce food. A regimented line of sweet corn runs along a side fence, and potato and beetroot leaves, onion sets and other evidence of nascent vegetables emerge from the rich dark soil. A line of sweet peppers is strung over the door to the house like a string of bright monotone Christmas lights. The rows of vines seem ripe to break under the weight of the purple garlands they bear. Tree branch wigwams of various heights are clad in French and runner and broad beans, and the tomatoes are almost the size of cannonballs. There is a rhubarb patch and a row of already sizeable pumpkins. A grove of fruit trees on the other side of the fence draws the eye towards the sloping ground and forest beyond. I can see plum and peach, fig, nectarine and apple and pear. Nearby is a huge wooden barrel sitting upright on blocks of stone, and a dozen brightly coloured beehives run along the back fence. Clearly, there will be no shortage of fruit and vegetables and alcoholic beverages in the house this winter. As Sally says, with the shop for bread and other ungrowable necessities, the villagers are almost self-sufficient.

There is no car on show, and, apart from the chickens, the only sign of life is what looks to be a very ancient donkey. It stands beside the sentry box toilet, regarding us with the lack of interest of the very old. Donkeys can live for fifty years, and Sally says this *magare* is claimed to be even older. If so, it is very fitting, as its owner is the oldest man in the village.

Andrei Andreev is thought to be approaching his hundredth year, though neither he nor his three daughters know his exact age. He was born in this house, is determined to die in it, and has hardly left the premises in decades. In fact it is thought he has not left the village for more than half a century. The reason for the trip was to visit a bar with a television in Berkovitsa to watch the safe return to earth of Yuri Gagarin after he became the first man in space. So moved by the occasion and the celebratory drinks was Andrei that he bought a foal in town and named it after the heroic Soviet cosmonaut. Unlike his namesake, Yuri is still alive, which in donkey's years means he, like his owner, has had a very long life indeed.

Sally says that the old man refuses to leave his home,

so the three daughters come to live with and look after him in shifts. Two will spend two days each here, and the one who draws the short straw will cover the rest of the week.

As we turn to leave, the door of the cottage opens and a thin, careworn-looking woman emerges and walks towards a line of washing strung between two of the fruit trees. She is wearing a wrap-round apron and, despite the weather, heavy boots. Her hair has been scraped up and formed into a tight bun on the top of her head. She looks resigned rather than bitter, and waves to us as she starts to unpeg a collarless striped shirt from the line.

Sally exchanges a few words with her, and reports that Andrei is as well as can be expected and as cantankerous as ever. The woman is his youngest daughter, and lives in Berkovitsa on her days off from caring for her father. She adds that all the daughters have tried to persuade Andrei to live with them, but he is adamant and they can see his point. All his memories of being a child, growing up and meeting and marrying his wife are here, and, as the daughters say, when you are old and have lost your spouse, you have nothing left but your memories.

~

About to follow Sally and Richard down to the car, I spot another property. It is a smaller version of Andrei's home, and sits at the very top of the track. It looks even more isolated because there is no fence or garden, and it has almost become part of the landscape.

When I ask about it, Sally looks a little embarrassed, and then says it is another of their properties. It has not been occupied since the death of old lady who lived there.

I ask if we can take a closer look, and we walk up the last hundred metres of track.

Although there are missing tiles and broken windows, the cottage looks sound. It sits at a sort of crossroads where the main track becomes two footpaths. One leads directly up through a copse to where the remains of the alleged Roman fort is to be found; the other disappears into the distance towards where the Planina mountain range marches eastwards.

I ask Sally why she had not mentioned this property, and she says that it, like the handbag designer's house, is not for sale. I enquire if that is because another member of the burgeoning art and crafts community has bought it, but she says no. It is just not for sale.

Without thinking to ask, I lift the wooden latch, push the door open and walk in, then quickly retreat as I am enveloped in a cascade of frantic fluttering and scrabbling. I close the door sharply, but not before I see a host of small creatures flying haphazardly around in the gloom.

Richard secures the latch as I recover, and Sally says I have disturbed the new residents. She explains that she and Richard bought the cottage from the daughter of the original occupant. The woman needed to sell it urgently to help pay for cancer treatment, so the sale was rushed through. Before work could begin, the cottage had become a maternity roost. In early summer, groups of pregnant bats seek somewhere safe to have their young. They gather together for the six to nine weeks of confinement, then suckle their pups for another month or so until they are ready to fly. The pups then venture out to forage for food. It is a very sensitive time, and the mothers may abandon a roost if they are disturbed. But it is late summer and the pups are now independent, so I have done no damage.

I apologise to the owners and the bat mothers, and ask what will happen now the youngsters are weaned. Will the couple make a start on renovation? Sally looks at her husband, then smiles and says no. Their tenants will be looking for somewhere to hibernate during the winter, and maternity colonies often return to the same roost year after year if it proves to be safe.

The little cottage would make a wonderful retreat for a member of the new artistic colony, but as far as she and her husband are concerned, the bat community has as much right to live there as any artist or writer.

Пазарните сили
Market forces

I have learned quite a few new Bulgarian words. This impressive selection of ways to tell someone to have sex with themselves comes about because of an interesting arrangement for traffic management on the outskirts of Montana.

Here the unsuspecting driver comes upon a five-way junction, with cars appearing to come from more directions than there are roads. To complicate matters, within this mini-spaghetti junction is a railway level crossing. Naturally and at whatever colour the lights are, the train takes absolute priority. As well as all this, the lights change in an eccentric pattern which seems to take no regard of how long any of the queues are, or the time they have been there. It is said to be said by some of the more superstitious Montanans that the junction is in fact the playground of the ancient Thracian gods, amusing themselves by trifling with the lives and fates of the mortals whose destinies they control. It is also not just foreigners or people who are unfamiliar with the town who fall foul of the system, which is why it is known locally as Russian Roulette corner.

The roads are especially busy today as it is Monday market day. There is a market of some sort every day in Montana, and I think you can tell a lot about a nation by its street markets. In France you can buy cheap and very vulgar clothing and very expensive foodstuffs. The flea markets are full of expensive old cooking pots and pans. At British boot sales you can buy cheap clothes pretending to be expensive ones, cloned movies and smuggled tobacco.

At today's market, you can buy a whole car, a whole distillery, some beautifully-executed religious paintings and lots of hunting and killing accessories.

It is said that you will find every component of every car made in Bulgaria for the last fifty years at today's market. Or you can buy a ready-assembled one. There is a line of respectable-looking vehicles near to the gates, and, like the other goods you can take one away if you have the cash.

We walk past a couple of curious assemblies of tightly-spiralling copper tubes, their vendors sitting on the floor beside them. One of the men is offering free samples of *Rakia* from a plastic bottle, and Richard says the man says his stillage and method of using it makes the best and strongest plum brandy in the country. The secret of how it is done comes with the price of the equipment.

Further on there is a huge display of agricultural implements and tools ranging from rusty scythes and sickles to a whole tractor; Then a row of stalls selling enough military clothing and kit to equip a small army. I see that most of the stalls and their owners are camouflaged. As elsewhere in Europe, fishermen and hunters like to dress as if they are intent on killing people.

In keeping with the mood is a row of stalls displaying clasp knives, daggers, hatchets and even swords. As we pass, I see a couple of policemen are examining a murderous-looking machete as they drink coffee and eat *kofte* burgers. They say something to the stallholder, who smiles, nods and passes them a small brown parcel. If it is a bribe I suspect it will be another burger, as I have yet to see a policeman not eating, drinking or smoking on duty. I have no statistics to prove it, but Bulgarian policemen must surely be amongst the fattest in Europe.

Beyond a line of bicycles and scooters in various stages of completeness, I pause to admire what must be the most incompetently stuffed fox in the country. Not only has the poor creature been shot in the prime of its life, but it has been sentenced to spend eternity looking like the result of one of Victor Frankenstein's earliest experiments. The body has obviously been constructed around a cylinder which is much longer than the original torso. The pipestem legs are without any defining features and are far too thin for the body, the eyes are made from buttons, and the poor creature faces an eternity of mockery with an understandably shocked expression.

Past a display of religious paintings promising an eternity in paradise is a virtual mountain of footwear. Trainers, shoes, sandals and high-heeled, platform, ankle and walking boots are piled indiscriminately to eye-level, and a dozen people are rooting through them. When someone finds a matching pair they like the look of, he or she will start the bargaining process with one of the tough-looking men who stand guard and make sure nobody absconds with a pair of plimsolls. Sally says that most of the contents of the pile will have come from boot sales in Britain. There, they would have sold for a pound or two, but will actually be worth more here. It is one of the anomalies of relative values in this country. You can pick up a house for the price of a designer handbag in the UK, but a pair of new shoes can set you back a week's wages.

Beyond boot hill, I see a sad Roma family sitting on a tarpaulin sheet. The man is wearing a sleeveless shirt and

I see he has a badly withered arm. The woman sits beside him, and their two children play with the selection of mostly useless items spread out on the sheet. The children seem happy and without a care; the adults sit silently and motionless, deliberately not looking up at passers-by. Amongst their offerings is a QUERTY keyboard with missing letters, and some mismatching items of cutlery. An Action Man with no head stands next to a colouring book which looks as if it has already been coloured. I see a pair of sandals which look roughly my size, give the woman a twenty leva note and hurry on. I feel no glow of smug or saintly self-satisfaction, but neither do I feel guilty of patronising them by paying at least double what they would have asked for the shoes. I can afford it, and the money will make their day and maybe their week a bit better.

~

I am back in Ivo's bad books, and because I have done more damage to the beloved Lada that he allows Richard to call his own.

It was a seriously hot day, and after a visit to the outdoor swimming baths at Berkovitsa I stopped off to stock up on cold beer at my favourite grocery store.

Surviving the journey back along the dual carriageway and through Komerinski, I had just waved to the stork family and the ladies' luncheon club when I lost sight of the way ahead because of the dense wall of steam emerging from under the bonnet. We struggled on uphill for another hundred yards, then the engine expired as I found the forbidden fifth gear.

A panic call and Ivo arrived with a length of tow-rope and the air of a nurse in a home for the incurably insane.

Another hour and Richard called to say that it was a broken fan belt which had caused the problem, and the Lada would be fixed by tomorrow. I was on probation, and would not be allowed to get behind the wheel again until I had passed a competence test with Ivo as the invigilator.

Any list of typical Bulgarian dishes would be incomplete without beetroot soup. This is how some of my Bulgarian friends make it:

Цвеклото супа
Tsvekloto supa
(beetroot soup)

Ingredients

Four cooked beetroots
An onion
Two cups of vegetable stock
Some vegetable oil
A tin of pulped tomatoes
100g crumbled sirene (feta-style cheese)
Seasoning

Method

1. Peel the beetroots and coarsely grate
2. Heat the oil in a pan and sauté the onions gently until soft
3. Add the beets and stock and bring to the boil
4. Add the tin of tomatoes and simmer for ten minutes
5. Season and serve after crumbling the cheese over

Bulgarians like their fish, but a lot of places are a long way from the sea. This is why freshwater fish dishes are so common. This is a simple way of serving up one of the most common species of sea fish:

лук скумрия
luk skumriya
(onion mackerel)

Ingredients

A kilogram of mackerel, cleaned and skinned and filleted
A large onion, sliced
A large tomato, sliced
A cup of cooking oil
Four tablespoons of chopped tomatoes
6 cloves of garlic
A lemon
Some breadcrumbs
A tablespoon of flour
Seasoning

Method

1. Gently sauté the sliced onion and garlic
2. Add the tomatoes and seasoning
3. Put the mix in a roasting tray
4. Add two cups of hot water
5. Cut the fillets into chunks and place on top
6. Arrange the sliced tomatoes on top of the fish
7. Add slices of lemon and sprinkle breadcrumbs over
8. Put in oven at medium heat
9. Carefully cook the flour in a saucepan with some oil and add some of the juices from the roasting tray
10. Pour the mix over the fish and roast until fish is tender (around a quarter of an hour)

Every September there is a festival of plums and what can be made with and from them in the central Bulgarian town of Troyan. This is a Bulgarian version of a famous sweetmeat named for a neighbouring country:

слива локумм
sliva lokum
(plum Turkish delight)

Ingredients

2 kilograms of plums
1 kilograms of sugar
200g finely crushed walnuts
Some dusting sugar

Method

1. After washing and cleaning and pitting, steam the plums
2. Rub them through a sieve
3. Mix the pulp with the sugar
4. Boil the mixture until it thickens
5. Before removing from heat, add the walnuts
6. Spread the mixture on a greased or lined baking tray 2 cm deep
7. Dry in a gentle oven
8. Cut into cubes and dust with sugar

My last day in Krasiva.

Sometimes a holiday romance can be with a place as well as a person, and both can be as fleeting. But I think this bond will last. It has been a truly memorable summer, and, no matter how facile it sounds, I have grown to feel comfortably at home amongst the people in this remarkable little Balkan village.

I breakfast on the roof while thinking how familiar the mountains and ever-changing sky and landscape have become in such a short time. This morning Kom is wreathed in a girdle of fluffy clouds, the Planina range is shrouded in a blue-grey mist and the air freshens as autumn approaches. Soon I will be in another world, and I am not sure I want to be there.

It is a good day to take a walk across the hills and say goodbye to Krasiva.

~

I pay my final tribute to the canine protection racketeers, then cross the lane and walk up the track to the upper forest. At the soaring wall of pine I think about taking on the challenge and going in search of the Roman fort, then hear a jingle of harness. I turn and see it is Old Ivan with his donkey.

The wagon is empty as it usually is, and I wonder if, like a retired car owner, he has nowhere in particular to go and just fancies a spin.

He pulls up and we exchange greetings and he talks and I pretend to listen. I have learned that Ivan is one of those sociable people who like to pass the time of day even though they know you do not understand what they are saying. I nod or shake my head at what I hope are appropriate junctures and he is sensible enough not to end any sentences with an obvious query which would require a verbal response. After several minutes of conversation I feel something trying to eat my shorts, and realise that the goat policeman is on duty.

We have not been introduced but Sally Moore tells me his name is Dimitar, and that he is probably the youngest resident in the village. He was a policeman in Berkovitsa, but when his wife died suddenly he took early retirement and came to live in the family home. Now he spends his days taking his goats on hugely long walks in the hills around the village. He has his own style of management and herding technique, but like Elenko, Ivan, Ivalin and the goat lady, he obviously has a deep love for his animals. Whereas the goat lady generally leaves her little herd to their own devices and Elenko constantly nags them like an exasperated mother, Dimitar puts on a stern manner which they clearly know to be an act. To me it seems their relationship to their animals is similar to the way people elsewhere often treat their pets as if they were humans. There is no such overt indulgence here, but it is easy to see how much affection is felt for goats and donkeys and dogs. This indulgence does not seem to extend to chickens, but perhaps this is because their owners eat them and their unborn young.

I leave the two men probably discussing the weather and their non-plans for the day, and walk on along the path which skirts the upper forest. Below me at the bottom of the slope lies the house of the oldest resident, and Yuri the donkey stands in his usual position by the log pile. I capture the moment with my camera and wonder how many more summers he will see, and how - if he goes first - it will affect his master.

A woman who is probably one of Andrei's three daughters is working in the miniature vineyard, and looks up as if she feels me watching her. I raise my staff, but she makes no response before bending back down to her work. It is coming up for the weekend, so perhaps she is not in a communicative mood because she has drawn the three-day shift.

The path joins up with the track, and I pause to admire the cottage of which the French handbag designer has made such a spectacular job. Sally says the lady has said she may move over to join the arts and crafts community permanently, and I wonder if that will happen and if the scheme will work. There is also the question of how any group brought together simply by a common interest can work. A 'community' used to refer to people who lived, by coincidence, in the same place. Nowadays everyone with any sort of similar background, ethnicity, job or even sexual orientation must be lumped together, regardless of where they live and who they are. As with the Pre-Raphaelites, this sort of arrangement can succeed when artists live and work in the same place, so perhaps the Arts & Crafts community of Krasiva will become as famous as Gauguin's Pont-Aven School in Brittany.

Whatever the outcome of Sally and Richard's scheme, this is certainly a perfect place for creative people to work. At worst it is a great place to have a really, really cheap holiday home.

The high track gradually descends to the lane and I walk around the rim of the valley to the village square.

Elenko's cart is parked outside the shop, and Kratzi is having a conversation with his donkey. Kratzi seems to be more relaxed in the company of animals, and Sally says it is rumoured that he sometimes goes into the forest to meet wild boar and even wolves.

In the store, I buy some bottled water and a box of chocolates for my neighbour to thank her for putting up with me, and Elenko translates. As he speaks no English I could have mimed to Madame direct, but I know he gets a sort of proprietary pleasure from acting as go-between. Before we leave, I ask him with an imaginary knife and fork and a point at the sky what he is doing for dinner, but he looks a little embarrassed and indicates that he has other things to do.

I wave to Kratzi and the donkey and walk across the square, past the communist monument and along the track which comes to an end overlooking the valley and lower forest.

I don't know if it is because this is the remotest part of the village, but it does seem that I am walking through time. There are no street lights, television aerials, cars or other symbols of modernity, and, because the communist cube project did not reach this far, the homes seem more diverse and characterful. It cannot be much fun to live in some of them when the winter bites, but as all film and television drama designers know, even the most cruelly deprived properties and areas can look appealing if set back far enough in the past.

I pass tiny shacks with corrugated iron roofs, half-ruined but obviously occupied stone, brick and mud cottages and the occasional comparatively substantial two-storey house. So far I have seen no humans, but chickens, ducks, goats and the odd cat go freely about their businesses. As custom demands, all dogs are banged up behind high fences.

Because the track takes the form of a promontory reaching out above the valley, the houses on either side have equally stunning views. All the gardens have vineyards and fruit trees and bushes and vegetable plots, and there is hardly a flower or ornamental plant on show. Flowers may please the western eye, but virtually everything growing in the gardens and groves and orchards in Krasiva is destined for eating or drinking.

As if they have come out to take a look at the passing stranger, I now encounter people as well as animals. A very old lady in headscarf and cardigan and long skirt hobbles up to her gate, and a man following a small group of goats stops, takes his hat off and wipes his brow, then shields his eyes from the sun to inspect me. On a porch, a very round old man sits on a broken chair and lifts a hand as I go by. As elsewhere in the village, there is no sign of children or young people, and I suddenly realise I am probably the youngest person within a dozen miles.

I run the gauntlet of curious but amiable inspection, pausing on occasion to take photographs. As courtesy demands, I hold my camera up to ask permission if there is someone near the properties I want to record. Nobody objects, but it is interesting that nobody poses when I aim the camera. They simply look incuriously into the lens, and I realise that the only other photograph some may have sat for would be their death notice.

Across the track, I see an elderly couple working in their garden with the mighty Planina range as a backdrop. He is reaching up into a tree, while she is nearby, bending over to work on the soil. It makes a perfect composition, so I steal a photograph, then move on. Moments later I hear someone calling, and look around to see the man pursuing me along the track. I prepare to defend myself and the camera, but he comes to a puffing stop some paces away and holds out a cupped hand. In it are two nectarines, literally bursting with ripeness. He uses his other hand to point at the sun, then wags his finger reprovingly. He is obviously admonishing me for not wearing a hat, so I lift a hand in acknowledgement and pull my ball cap from the rucksack.

He waits till I put the cap on, then points at the pieces

of fruit. I take one and bite into it and juice runs down my chin. He smiles, shakes his head in satisfaction and turns and walks back to his garden. Such simple acts of kindness are worth so much more here.

A little further on and I come upon the first car I have seen since leaving the square. Almost inevitably, it is a Lada. It makes Richard's model look pristine, and its working days are clearly over. The tyres are on the rims and the windscreen and wing mirrors long gone. I take a closer look and there is a squawk of resentment from the hen taking its ease on a pile of straw on the back seat. Doffing my cap in apology, I walk on to where a pile of stones makes a seat with a wonderful view across the valley. Sitting there, I wonder for the hundredth time how it would be to live in such a place, and not just for a few weeks. The villagers know no other life, of course. They have always lived here and not somewhere where all streets are paved, shops are to hand, and all toilets indoors.

Like many people, my wife and I always loved the idea of escaping urban life. We have lived in remote places, but for short periods of time, knowing we would be returning to the benefits as well as the noise and clamour of city life. Here, there is peace and solitude at a risible price, but I wonder if we would be able to detox ourselves of the cravings for such commonplace facilities as convenience stores and flushable lavatories. Roger seems to have found contentment here, but he has done it by surrounding himself with all the comforts, gadgets and toys of urban living. In the process he has created a little outpost of England and can live at a fraction of the costs back home. But the price is that he must live alone.

I finish off the other nectarine and prepare to walk back to the guest house. I don't know if I could live the really simple life here or anywhere, and perhaps I am too fearful to find out.

~

The expanse of glittering silver has drawn me across country for nearly a mile, but now I see it is only the tin roof of a huge building. From my elevated vantage point I can see there are no windows, and its angular, bleak lines look strangely out of place in the sylvan surroundings. Several vehicles are in the yard, but no sign of human activity. I scramble downhill and reach within a hundred yards of the mystery building before I recognise the Range Rover with a missing wing mirror. It is Mr Big's car, and this must be the place where they raise the sheep destined for the family butchery in Berkovitsa.

Arriving at the fenceless perimeter of the yard, I stop suddenly as I hear the bellowing of an angry bull and something massive appears from behind the Range Rover. It is neither an angry bull nor Mr Big, but going by its size and appearance it can only be his dog.

After the wing mirror incident, Ivalin explained that Mr Big's family is of an ancient race called Karakachans, who were nomadic shepherds and horse breeders. The race gave its name to a breed of huge mountain dogs, now used for guarding livestock, property and people. This one is about the size of a smallish pony, but looks much more dangerous and unfriendly.

I gulp a few times and try to make myself look not worth the trouble of attacking. The monster regards me with its head on one side as if considering whether to greet or eat me, then more roaring fills the air. There is a panting and pawing of the ground as another even bigger creature emerges from behind the Range Rover. I gulp some more as I realise that my original confrontation was with the runt of the litter. The second dog is as big as a big pony, and even more unfriendly-looking than the first one.

We stand our ground while I wonder whether it would be best to fight or take flight. I have decided on the latter when there is a sharp whistle, the sun is blotted out and

Mr Big appears. He looks at me quizzically, then says something to the dogs. They slink off back behind the car, and he raises a giant hand of acknowledgement. I return his greeting, then back away into the treeline. When out of sight I will find somewhere to recover, have a coffee and check on the condition of my boxer shorts.

~

Dusk steals across the valley, and I am home alone.

It is my last evening in Krasiva and Bulgaria, but nobody to spend it with except Muttley and the lizard which has set up home in the old cooking range on the balcony.

Sally and Richard are committed to dining with friends in Berkovitsa, and Roger said he is going to Montana with Ivo to pick up his new dog. I can't go for a drink at the local because there isn't one, and the road to Berkovitsa is dangerous enough without having even one glass of fine Bulgarian Zorzal Chardonnay.

I have settled for a chapter or two of *Travels with my Donkey* by Robert Louis Stevenson, a home-made mish-mash with bubble and squeak overtones, and a bottle of Ivalin's strawberry *Rakia*, but would rather have spent my last evening in company.

I decide to go for a final walk across the hills, and in search of what sounds an intriguing property. Roger says that Ivo says there is an empty villa on the other side of the upper forest. It is surrounded by vineyards, and he does not know if it is for sale, as the doctor who used it as a holiday home died some time ago. He lived and practiced in another province, and nobody knows if he has any relatives or who or where they are.

I have failed to find the alleged Roman fort above the forest, but a villa in the middle of a vineyard should be less of a challenge. I kit myself out with my headband light and a back-up torch, and take a cold *banitsa* and add a tot of *Rakia* to my coffee flask in case I become lost and have to spend the night in the open.

~

To most people, a villa would suggest a cool home in a hot place. It would ideally have extensive grounds and a pool and may even be principally constructed of highly polished marble.

In Bulgaria, a villa may be made of stone, wood or tin and is supposed to be a temporary dwelling place built in the countryside without the need for planning permission. It is also supposed to be without water and electricity, but some people cheat. Вила means 'villa', but can equally mean a proper country house, a summerhouse or a pitchfork for shifting dung.

This Вила is silhouetted against the darkening sky and my pulse quickens as I climb the footpath up from the track which leads down to the lane going through the village. My shortness of breath and increase in heart rate is not just because of my poor condition and the height of my destination. The setting and the place are just so perfect, and before reaching it I know we are made for each other.

And this in spite of all my experience in these matters. After years of searching out and messing around with remote and ruined properties in France, I have found that it is rarely a good idea to make such an early judgement, especially from a distance. When you arrive it may be that the property backs on to a busy road or is sited next door to an abattoir. Or it might just be that the place does not live up to the fantastical image you have imposed on it.

But this is different. As I reach the top of the hill, the prospects get better and better.

The villa is of solid brick and block and on two storeys with a steeply-pitched roof of corrugated iron. Some might see this as a downside, but, though noisy when it rains, hot in summer and sometimes freezing in winter, a solid tin roof can be better than a leaky old tile one. And it would not be expensive to re-roof it, though Ivo could have a problem getting the materials up the footpath.

I walk around the building, past the outdoor toilet and then back to the front, where the ground slopes away and gives access to the basement. A pristine wrought-iron staircase leads to the first floor and two large rooms, accessed by a balcony which runs the width of the house. The windows and glass in the doors are undamaged, and there is no sign of vandalism or illicit occupation, which is another good sign. One room holds a heating and cooking stove and a sink and a rough table with a couple of rickety chairs. The other has a single bed with a high head and tailboard. Near it are a small table and two raffia-seated chairs and a water jug and glass. Perhaps I am being over-imaginative, but the way the chairs are angled and the bed is set against one wall puts me in mind of the painting of Van Gogh's bedroom in Arles.

From the balcony and enhanced by the failing light, the view is simply stunning.

The villa sits at the highest point of the highest hill in the vicinity, and the slopes are completely covered with rows of vines. From the south-facing balcony, the whole panoply of the Planina range fills the horizon and the peaks seem to reach to the first stars of the evening. Directly beyond the vineyard is the valley, and on either side are undulating hills fringed with woods and the beginnings of the upper forest. I put my hands on the balcony rail and take a deep breath of the autumnal air and imagine what it would be like to have this as a writer's retreat. Far away in the valley, a bonfire burns and smoke curls lazily upwards. I imagine I can smell the fragrance, and I can certainly hear the clanking of the bells around the necks of the Berkovitsa collective cow herd.

Not so long ago I would have abandoned whatever I was doing and focused on nothing else but making this magical place mine. Nowadays, I am and need to be more circumspect.

Tomorrow I will ask Sally to call Ivo and ask if he will do some detective work to find out who now owns the villa and if it is for sale. If it is, my credit card will be ready.

~

I have hardly set foot on the lane at the bottom of the hill on which the villa stands when I am blinded by a single headlight. It is attached to Ivalin's works bus, and he brings it screaming to a stop a few inches from my left boot.

He beckons me to get in, and says he has been looking for me. I ask why and he replies that he wants me to look at his house. I say it is dark, and I have anyway seen his house. He looks at me as if I am simple and says the house he wants me to look at is not the house he lives in. It is the house he was born in. As he speaks, he crunches the gearstick into approximately the right socket, I shut my eyes and we are off.

Three stomach-churning minutes later, and in spite of what he said about not going to the house he lives in we pull up outside it. I climb shakily down and wave to Petar and Kratzi, who are sitting in the debating shelter. Ivalin also gets out of his van and beckons me to follow him. I say the other house can't be far if we are going on foot, and before I finish saying it, we are there.

The communist cube lookalike is set back from the dirt lane alongside Ivalin's present house, and one side is holding up the barn in which Kratzi lodges.

Ivalin pushes open the high metal gate, while I switch on my headlamp and we force our way through man-high grass, weeds, bushes, plants and shrubs to the steps. Even though it is dark I can see that the garden is enormous and slopes down towards the bottom of the valley.

I compliment him on the location and the vineyard, and he absent-mindedly picks a grape and says it is sad that the house and garden are no longer being looked after. He explains that he was born here after his father built the house, and until last year his elderly aunt would stay for the summer and keep the grounds in order. Now she is too old and frail to make the journey from Sofia, so the house needs a new owner. It is against his better judgement because he already has one mad person living next door, but if I want it I can have it.

I say I am flattered that he would want me as a neighbour and that I would like to look inside. He says he has lost the keys, but if I come to his other house he will look for them.

Johnny's joyous bark greets us as Ivalin opens the gate; He fiddles with the door and, for the first time since we met, invites me in to his home.

~

I suppose I should have been suspicious when all my new friends declared themselves busy for my last night in Krasiva. Also that there were two donkeys in the space in the garden where there is usually one.

As I follow Ivalin into the main room, a bagpipe drone strikes up, followed by a somehow very Slavic version of *For He's a Jolly Good Fellow*.

Seated at the big pine table are Sally and Richard, Roger and Elenko. The chairs at each end are unoccupied, and Ivo is standing at one with a tray containing a small dish, a loaf and a full tumbler of what can only be strawberry or raspberry *Rakia*.

Ivalin calls for silence, and looking even more President Putin-like, makes a very short address.

It is, he tells us, an old Bulgarian custom to meet an important visitor with a gift of salt and bread. When he heard I was coming to Krasiva, he did not think I was important enough to be given the honour. He is still not sure how important I am and if my book will be good for the village, but he thinks the village likes me. I have tried to fit in and not act like a rich foreigner, even though that is what I am. He and the rest of the gathering hope that I have enjoyed my stay in Krasiva and will write good things about the village and the people. If my book makes him and the village and its people famous that will not be too bad, as they will all be able to sell their homes for a great deal of money. That is if Sally and Richard have not bought them all already.

So before we eat, we will toast Krasiva, the Balkans, Bulgaria...and the fate that brought us together. He ends by saying that he hopes it will not be too long before I return.

I find the last fly of summer has got into my eye, and after attending to it, I lift my glass and say that nothing, not bears nor boars, nor wolves nor even Ivalin's driving will keep me away.

It seems Bulgaria does not want me to leave.

Milen picked me and my Grade Four hangover up at dawn and said he was early because we needed to collect some other passengers with reason to be in Sofia that day.

Climbing the path from the guest house for the last time I saw that Muttley and Jeff and the other gang members were sitting in the road, watching me glumly. I had no need to pay tribute today, but threw them my last Curly-Wurly bar before climbing in the Galaxy.

As well as every pothole, I think Milen must know the majority of the fourteen thousand people who currently live in Berkovitsa. This may be because the very low car ownership means they are regular customers. Today, we picked up an elderly couple, a sleepy-eyed woman who looked as if she had spent the night somewhere she should not have been, and a stick-thin young student in the universal uniform of trainers, ripped jeans, tee-shirt and earphones. The power of fashion was ironically demonstrated by the way someone from the poorest country in Europe would pay extra to have jeans with holes in them.

7.12 a.m.:

All went very smoothly as we climbed the first of the corkscrew ups and downs of the mountain pass. With Milen translating, the elderly couple were asking about life in England, the student was concentrating on the buzzing in his ears, and the young woman was looking out of the window and obviously thinking about somewhere or someone else.

Then, just as we reached the peak, the engine coughed and spluttered and died and the dashboard went into meltdown. Lights flashed, sirens wailed tinnily, and a voice sounding very like the robot in *Lost in Space* said the Bulgarian equivalent of 'Warning, Warning. We are about to collide with a rogue asteroid.'

Luckily there was a layby for Milen to turn into before gravity took its effect, and he put the handbrake on, got out and approached the front of the car in a decidedly determined manner. I don't know if the over-the-top alarm sequence is a regular occurrence, but the passengers seemed unperturbed and it is only me who surreptitiously checked the time.

7.31a.m.:

To the best of my recollection, there are around half a dozen major ups and downs on the mountain pass road before it is downhill most of the way to the elevated plain on which Sofia sits.

We reached the third before the dashboard erupted again and the engine conked out. This time, Milen reached into the glove box and took out a small hammer and clasp knife before stalking to the bonnet and opening it. Through the windscreen, I could see his lips moving and it seemed to me he was giving the engine a Basil Fawlty ultimatum.

Post and even pre-communist era lorries wheezed by unconcernedly as he completed the repairs before returning to the driver's seat. The threat worked, as the engine started and we set off again.

9.42 a.m.:

After a heart-in-mouth journey for me if nobody else on board, Milen has coaxed the Galaxy to the capital, dropped the other passengers in the centre and we are now sitting outside the airport. The engine has been hiccupping and threatening to cut out for the past forty seven miles, and now it has.

I thank him for getting me here on time and when I ask what he will do about fixing the car, he gives a very Bulgarian shrug. He knows people, he says, and he will get a friend to bring a tow rope. I pay him and include a tip to cover the cost of the rescue mission and the parts which may be needed, and we shake hands. I say it is the third time I have been in a car which has had engine trouble since I arrived, and he smiles and says then it is all for the best. It is well known that these things happen in threes, and it is better for his car's engine to break down rather than the one in the Easyjet plane.

We soar up and away from Sofia, and I look down on the now-familiar work-in-progress buildings as I think about the last three months in this fascinating land.

I don't remember ever settling in and feeling so at home anywhere in such a short time, and it is a curious and even a little disappointing feeling to realise that life will go on in Krasiva exactly as it did before I arrived. After I am gone, all will be exactly as it was before I came, and as if I had never been. Ivalin will continue driving madly across the countryside with his cargo of Roma ladies. Old Ivan and Angel will continue to meet on their donkey carts as they go for their daily spins. The goat lady and policeman and Elenko will continue to chide their beloved animals as they do the rounds of near and distant feeding stations. Roger will continue to live his transferred life, and Sally and Richard will pursue their dream of bringing new life to the village by creative foreign investment. I must go back to where I came from and try to come up with a fairly accurate and hopefully engaging account of what I found in the beautiful village of Krasiva and that part of the Balkans.

Sitting next to me on the flight to Gatwick is a large lady in her middle years. She has been watching me watching Sofia disappear with an open but inoffensive curiosity which I have learned is another typically Bulgarian trait.

She holds out a big bag of sweets and when I politely decline, she says I should not be so English. She can see just by looking at me that I like sweet things, so why would I refuse a free candy? I think about her Bulgarian logic and, finding it inarguable, agree and take one. We suck and chew contentedly for a while, then she asks me who I am, where I have been and why.

When I tell her, she presses another sweet on me and says she owns a house in Berkovitsa and hopes to retire there. For now, she and her husband live and work at a care home in Eastbourne, which seems to have a higher percentage of old people living there than where I have been for the past three months.

I ask her what she thinks of what she has seen of England, and she gives a so-so Bulgarian shrug. My country is, she says, exactly what she thought it would be like. A rich country with lots of rich people who do not know how lucky they are. When I ask her how she feels about the number of Britons moving to live in her country, she laughs and says there has been a joke doing the rounds that only old and poor British people come to live in Bulgaria. Now that Britain is leaving the European Union there will be a lot more, and it is said the Roma fruit pickers are worried about the possible competition. Personally she thinks that the invasion of Britons is preferable to previous occupations by Turks and Communists.

After showing me lots of photographs of her recent holiday in Africa, Ana opens a giant packet of crisps and leaves me to think why so relatively few Britons have chosen to come to live in her country.

Perhaps things will change and Bulgaria will become the next hot-spot for British expats, and I cannot honestly think why this would not be so. I have travelled in many countries, and, based on my time in this part of their country, I find myself particularly drawn to everyday Bulgarians.

I think this is partly because I admire their resilience and determination to make the best of things. It seems to me that they are at the same time inclined towards but reluctant to accept what fate and their leaders have brought them. Successive governments and regimes have made bad choices, and it has always been the ordinary people who have ended up with the shitty end of the stick.

Whatever else, it has been a fascinating summer in a place which has been both alien and familiar. With its landscape, history and culture and the way ordinary people take on life and what it throws at them, I have found Bulgaria to a bewitching country; for sure, it will not be long before I return.

Learning more about Bulgaria

Tourism is a major source of revenue for Bulgaria and contributes 15 percent of the country's GDP. More than eleven million visitors arrive each year, which might not sound a big deal when compared with hotspots like France and Spain. It is more impressive a figure when you consider that nearly twice as many tourists visit the country than the people who live there.

The Official Tourist portal of Bulgaria can be found at:-
http://bulgariatravel.org/

The website for the Ministry of Tourism is at:-
http://www.tourism.government.bg/en

I found the Wikipedia Voyage entry dealing with Bulgaria very helpful as a sort of Reader's Digest guide to the history, topography, structure and modern attractions of Bulgaria. Have a look at:-
https://en.wikivoyage.org/wiki/Bulgaria

As noted in the book, there always seems to be something to celebrate in Bulgaria. The country has many sometimes curious traditions and special days, from chasing away evil spirits on New Year's Eve to depositing umbilical cords in places which will determine a child's future career and success. Many more fascinating facts can be found at:-
https://www.justlanded.com/english/Bulgaria/Bulgaria-Guide/Culture/Curious-Bulgarian-traditions

The above website also carries a helpful guide to what to do and where to go in Sofia.

Bibliography

Before going to Bulgaria I got through a veritable shedload of books, travel guides and websites. This is a selection of those I found most useful, informative or just enjoyable:

Travel guides

The Rough Guide to Bulgaria by Jonathan Bousfield and Dan Richardson. **www.roughguides.com**

Bulgaria: Eyewitness Travel. **www.traveldk.com**

Bulgaria: Insight Guides.
amazon.bulgaria+insight+guide

Bulgaria: Lonely Planet. **www.lonelyplanet.com**

Bulgaria Tour Guide by Kapka Nikolova. More info at **www.bgbook.dir.bg**

The Lonely Planet Bulgarian phrasebook & dictionary. **www.lonelyplanet.com**

Information & non-fiction books:

Neither Here nor There: Travels in Europe by Bill Bryson (1991)

The Mountains of Bulgaria (a walker's companion) by Julian Perry.

Who were the Thracians? by Nenko Bererov (Plovdiv 2007)

The Shortest History of Bulgaria by Nicolav Ovcharov. (Lettera 2006)

Buying a property in Bulgaria by Jonathan White. **amazon./Buying-Property-Bulgaria**

The Bulgarians. Edited by Prof/Dr/Sc. Alexander Fol

Fiction

Under the Yoke by Ivan Vazov.
amazon.co.uk/Under the Yoke by Ivan Vazov

Solo by Rana Dasgupta
www.goodreads-solo

Valley of Thracians
amazon.co.uk/Valley of the Thracians-by Ellis-Shuman

More Books about Bulgaria at:-

www.goodreads.com Books_about_Bulgaria

www.amazon.co.uk-bulgarian books

For further information visit George's website at **www.george-east.net** and read more about his Bulgarian exploits and other European adventures.

Printed in Great Britain
by Amazon